AI for Ministry

Transforming Faith in

the Digital Age

Jeremy Wheeler

with Bill Scheidler

2

Published by: Independently published

ISBN (Paperback): 9798264487583

Printed on demand.

Trademarks: All trademarks and product names are the property of their respective owners and are used for identification purposes only.

Scripture acknowledgments (include only the translations actually used):

Cover design: Jeremy Wheeler

Editing: Jeremy Wheeler and Bill Scheidler

Permissions/Contact: https://smartaicoach.com

Acknowledgments

I am profoundly grateful to Pastor Bill Scheidler for his invaluable contribution to this book. Bill generously offered his time and expertise to edit and proofread the manuscript, driven by his belief in this project. His insightful guidance and profound understanding have significantly enhanced the quality and depth of this work.

Bill is a respected pastor, author, and teacher who has dedicated his life to Christian education and ministry training. His numerous published works—including The Local Church Today, Apostles, the Fathering Servant, Growing Strong Churches, Principles of Church Life, Watch Out for Wolves—have enriched the lives of countless believers and leaders around the world. In addition, his three manuals for discipleship, including Next Step 1.0, 2.0, and 3.0 have been used by many as convenient tools to deepen the spiritual lives of the people of God.

Passionate about equipping pastors and leaders, Bill founded the School of Ministry, aiming at empowering churches to disciple, train, and equip their own teams within the church, by the church, and for the church. He believes that the local church should be the primary place where leaders are prepared and released into ministry. Recognizing that many pastors lack accessible or affordable resources, Bill provides high-quality materials—often for free or at minimal cost—through his website: www.churchleadershipresources.com.

I also express my deep appreciation to Timothy Dean Johnson, whose visionary idea of creating an easy-to-understand book on AI has been the cornerstone of this project. His enthusiasm and commitment to making complex technological concepts accessible have been a driving force behind bringing this book to fruition.

Together, Bill and Timothy embody the incredible ways God can use dedicated individuals to impact the world. Their commitment to embracing innovation while staying rooted in faith has encouraged me to explore the transformative potential of technology in ministry. I am thankful for their guidance, vision, and the way the Holy Spirit has moved through them to make this project possible.

May this work serve as a testament to what God can achieve through us when we are open to His leading, combining timeless truths with modern tools to reach a world in need.

Table of Contents

Foreword

We are living in very interesting times where things seem to be moving at warp speed on so many different fronts. For those who are familiar with Bible prophecy, it seems that many of the predictions of the prophets of old and Jesus Himself are coming to pass. It makes one wonder if we are rapidly moving into the last of the last days.

One such area of acceleration is in the field of AI technology. As with so many significant advances in technology, this entry into the world of AI presents both challenges and opportunities. On the one hand, it presents challenges in the realm of the misuse of AI to advance the purposes of our spiritual enemy—the devil. But, on the other hand, it opens unbelievable opportunities for the advancement of the Gospel and the extension of the Kingdom of God and the purposes of God in the earth today.

Oftentimes, when these profound advances occur we can find ourselves being critical or even resisting the use of such technologies. We do this because we allow our imagination to go wild in areas of potential abuse. However, if we would allow our minds to be expanded by focusing on the potential for use in positive ways, especially when it comes to fulfilling the Great Commission, we could get very excited.

When we do begin to see the potential in AI for achieving lofty purposes, we will want to embrace it and begin to take full advantage of it in our ministries. AI can assist us in becoming more efficient. It can assist us in the things that can bog us down in administration freeing us to focus on true, Holy Spirit-directed ministry. There are ways that it can assist us in every department of the local church, including our outreach and missionary activity.

For us to reap the benefits, however, we must be willing to learn and draw from the expertise of others. Enter Jeremy Wheeler. Jeremy is a trained professional in the area of AI who also has a heart for God and the work of God in the earth. His vision is to assist the Body of Christ by equipping it to be able to stay current, relevant, and fully armed to meet the demands of the world of today.

In this book you will see how AI, used properly in conjunction with hearts and minds who are led and directed by the Holy Spirit, can assist and even enhance all of the work that God has called us to do. For this reason I have engaged with him to see this project come to pass. I would also recommend his companion work, AI for Novices.

I encourage you to read and be challenged and inspired. Remember in this book we will present what can be done, it is up to you to decide if it should be done in each specific area of ministry.

Bill Scheidler, Church Leadership Resources

Preface

In the rapidly evolving 21st-century landscape, the Church finds itself at a critical juncture. As artificial intelligence (AI) reshapes virtually every aspect of our society, from commerce to communication, from entertainment to education, we, as leaders in ministry, are called to engage with this transformative technology thoughtfully. It is with this sense of urgency and opportunity that I present "AI in Ministry: The Intersection of Faith and Technology."

The Apostle Paul's words in 1 Corinthians 9:22-23 have long guided the Church's approach to cultural engagement: "I have become all things to all people so that by all possible means I might save some. I do all this for the sake of the gospel that I may share in its blessings." In our current context, engaging with AI represents one of the "means" by which we can effectively minister in our increasingly digital world.

However, our engagement with AI must be grounded in biblical wisdom and discernment. As Proverbs 4:7 reminds us, "The beginning of wisdom is this: Get wisdom. Though it cost all you have, get understanding." This book aims to provide that wisdom and understanding, offering a comprehensive exploration of AI's potential applications in ministry, as well as the theological and ethical considerations that must guide its use.

The genesis of this book lies in my own journey of grappling with the implications of AI for ministry. As a pastor and technology enthusiast, I found myself both excited by the possibilities AI presents and cautious about its potential pitfalls. I realized that many of my colleagues in ministry were wrestling with similar questions: How can we leverage AI to enhance our ministry efforts without compromising our values or the essential human and spiritual elements of our work? How do we navigate the ethical challenges posed by AI? What does responsible stewardship of this technology look like in a ministry context?

These questions led me on a path of research, reflection, and practical experimentation. This book is the fruit of that journey, synthesizing insights from theology, technology, and practical ministry experience. It is designed to be a comprehensive resource for pastors, ministry leaders, and anyone interested in the intersection of faith and AI.

In these pages, you will find a balanced approach to AI in ministry. We will explore this technology's exciting possibilities for enhancing our work in areas such as pastoral care, sermon preparation, worship, administration, and outreach. At the same time, we will critically examine the challenges and potential risks, always grounding our discussion in biblical principles and the rich tradition of Christian thought.

This book is not just a theoretical exploration. It is designed to be a practical guide, offering concrete strategies for implementing AI in various ministry contexts. Whether you lead a small rural church or a large urban congregation, whether you're tech-savvy or a digital novice, you will find insights and guidance relevant to your situation.

Isaiah 43:19, "See, I am doing a new thing!" comes to mind as we begin this exploration together. Now it springs up; do you not perceive it? "I am making a way in the wilderness and streams in the wasteland." AI represents a "new thing" in our ministerial landscape. It is my prayer that this book will help you perceive the opportunities it presents and navigate the challenges it poses, always advancing God's kingdom and glorifying Him in all we do.

It's important to note that this book does not advocate for the wholesale adoption of AI in ministry. Rather, it is a call for thoughtful, prayerful engagement with this technology. As the theologian Abraham Kuyper famously said, "There is not a square inch in the whole domain of our human existence over which Christ, who is Sovereign over all, does not cry, Mine!" This includes the domain of artificial intelligence. Our task is to discern how to acknowledge and implement Christ's lordship in this new frontier.

The structure of this book is designed to take you on a journey from understanding the basics of AI and its relevance to ministry through practical applications in various areas of church life to considering the future implications and ethical challenges of this technology. Each chapter builds on the previous ones, providing a comprehensive framework for engaging with AI in ministry.

I encourage you to approach this book with an open mind and a discerning spirit. As you read, continually ask yourself, How might these insights apply in my specific ministry context? What opportunities does AI present for enhancing our ability to serve God and our community? What potential pitfalls must we be aware of and guard against?

Remember, the goal is not to become experts in AI technology but to become wise stewards of this powerful tool. As we navigate this new terrain, may we be guided by the wisdom of Proverbs 3:5-6: "Trust in the Lord with all your heart and lean not on your own understanding; in all your ways submit to him, and he will make your paths straight."

It is my sincere hope that this book will equip you to engage confidently and effectively with AI in your ministry, always keeping your focus on our ultimate purpose: to glorify God and make disciples of all nations. May our exploration of this new frontier in technology deepen our wonder at God's creativity, sharpen our effectiveness in ministry, and ultimately draw us and those we serve into a closer relationship with our Creator.

As we begin this journey together, I invite you to join me in prayer, asking for God's wisdom and guidance as we seek to faithfully navigate the intersection of faith and technology in service of His kingdom.

At His feet,

Jeremy Wheeler

Introduction

The Intersection of Faith and Technology: A Christian Perspective

In an era where digital innovation permeates every aspect of our lives, the Christian faith and modern technology converge in unprecedented ways. This intersection presents both exciting opportunities and profound challenges for followers of Christ worldwide. As we stand at the threshold of a new technological age, believers must engage thoughtfully with these advancements, considering how they might enhance our spiritual practices while remaining true to our core beliefs in Jesus Christ, the guidance of the Holy Spirit, and the sovereignty of God the Father.

Biblical Foundations: Faith and Human Innovation

The relationship between faith and human innovation is deeply rooted in Scripture. From the very beginning, we see God as the ultimate Creator, forming the universe and all that is in it (Genesis 1-2). Humanity, created in God's image, is endowed with the capacity for creativity and innovation. This divine spark of creativity reflects our Creator's nature and forms part of our calling to be stewards of God's creation.

Throughout the Bible, we see examples of God-inspired innovation:

1. Noah's Ark (Genesis 6-9): A massive engineering project guided by divine instruction.
2. The Tabernacle and later Solomon's Temple (Exodus 25-31, 1 Kings 6): Intricate designs blending artistry and functionality for worship.

3. Nehemiah's rebuilding of Jerusalem's walls
    (Nehemiah 2-6): A feat of organization and
    construction.

These narratives remind us that the ability to create and innovate is part of our divine nature, reflecting the image of God, the Creator, in humanity. As the Apostle Paul reminds us, "For we are God's handiwork, created in Christ Jesus to do good works, which God prepared in advance for us to do" (Ephesians 2:10, NIV).

The Digital Revolution and Christian Ministry

The advent of the internet and digital technologies has ushered in a new era of possibilities for Christian ministry. Online platforms have enabled global connectivity, allowing believers to access Biblical teachings, participate in virtual worship services, and engage in faith-based discussions across geographical boundaries. Social media has become a powerful tool for evangelism and community building, while smartphone apps offer daily devotionals, prayer reminders, and Bible study tools at our fingertips.

These digital tools have proven particularly valuable during times of crisis, such as the COVID-19 global pandemic of 2020, when many churches were forced to adapt quickly to online formats. The ability to stream services, conduct virtual Bible studies, and provide pastoral care through video calls has demonstrated the resilience and adaptability of the Body of Christ in the face of unprecedented challenges.

Yet, as we embrace these technologies, we must also consider their impact on the nature of the Christian experience and community. Does a virtual church service provide the same sense of communal worship as an in-person gathering? How do we maintain the sanctity of sacred spaces and rituals in a digital environment? These are questions that Christian leaders and communities must grapple with as we navigate the digital landscape, always seeking to honor the instruction in Hebrews 10:25 (NIV): "Not giving up meeting together, as some are in the habit of doing, but encouraging one another—and all the more as you see the Day approaching."

Artificial Intelligence and Christian Spirituality

As we delve deeper into the 21st century, artificial intelligence (AI) emerges as a frontier technology that holds both promise and peril for Christian communities. AI has the potential to revolutionize many aspects of ministry and spiritual practice. From chatbots that can provide 24/7 pastoral support to AI-powered tools for biblical exegesis and sermon preparation, the applications are vast and varied.

However, the rise of AI also raises profound theological and ethical questions. As we create machines that can think and learn, we must consider what it means to be human, created in God's image (Genesis 1:27). How does our understanding of the soul, consciousness, and free will align with these technological advancements?

Moreover, as AI becomes more sophisticated in generating human-like text and even creative works, we must grapple with questions of authorship and inspiration. If an AI system can write a compelling sermon or compose a beautiful worship song, how do we discern the role of the Holy Spirit in these acts? We are reminded of Paul's words in 1 Corinthians 2:13 (NIV): "This is what we speak, not in words taught us by human wisdom but in words taught by the Spirit, explaining spiritual realities with Spirit-taught words."

Ethical Considerations Through a Christian Lens

The integration of technology into Christian practices brings forth a host of ethical considerations. Privacy concerns are paramount, especially when dealing with sensitive personal information shared in pastoral care settings or through faith-based apps. The use of data analytics to tailor religious messages or predict individual spiritual needs raises questions about manipulation and the authenticity of personal faith journeys.

As Christians, we must approach these ethical dilemmas with wisdom and discernment, guided by biblical principles. Jesus' teaching to be "as shrewd as snakes and as innocent as doves" (Matthew 10:16, NIV) takes on new meaning in the digital age. We must be tech-savvy enough to understand and utilize these tools effectively yet maintain our integrity and commitment to truth and love.

Additionally, the digital divide – the gap between those who have access to technology and those who do not – presents a challenge for churches seeking to embrace digital tools. How can we ensure that technological advancements in ministry do not inadvertently exclude or marginalize certain members of our communities? This concern echoes the early church's commitment to caring for all members of the body, as seen in Acts 6:1-7.

Balancing Tradition and Innovation in Christian Practice

One of the central challenges at the intersection of faith and technology is striking a balance between honoring Christian traditions and embracing innovation. Many churches find themselves navigating between two extremes: those who resist any technological change, fearing it will dilute or distort sacred practices, and those who eagerly adopt every new technology without critical evaluation.

The key lies in thoughtful discernment guided by the Holy Spirit. Christian leaders and communities must carefully consider how each technological tool aligns with core Biblical values and the mission of the church. This requires a deep understanding of both the technology itself and the theological implications of its use. It also calls for ongoing dialogue within faith communities to ensure that technological adoption serves to enhance, rather than replace, meaningful spiritual experiences and human connections.

As we navigate this balance, we can draw inspiration from Paul's approach of becoming "all things to all people" for the sake of the gospel (1 Corinthians 9:22, NIV), while also heeding the warning not to conform to the pattern of this world but be transformed by the renewing of our minds (Romans 12:2).

A Journey of Faith and Innovation

As we embark on this exploration of faith and technology, we stand at the cusp of a new era in Christian ministry and practice. The pages that follow will delve deeper into the various facets of this intersection, examining how artificial intelligence, digital platforms, and emerging technologies are reshaping our approach to worship, evangelism, pastoral care, and community building.

We will wrestle with challenging questions, explore innovative applications, and seek to discern a path forward that honors our timeless faith while embracing the tools of our time. Through it all, we will be guided by the unchanging truths of Scripture and the living presence of the Holy Spirit, ever mindful of our calling to be salt and light in an increasingly digital world.

As we turn the page to the next chapter, let us approach this journey with open minds, discerning hearts, and a steadfast commitment to glorifying God in all things – even in the realm of bits and bytes.

CHAPTER ONE

The Intersection of Faith and Technology

Section 1.1: How Faith and Technology Have Historically Intersected

As we embark on this exploration of artificial intelligence in ministry, it's crucial to understand the historical context of how faith and technology have intersected throughout the ages. This journey through time will reveal a rich tapestry of innovation, adaptation, and sometimes tension as God's people have grappled with new tools and ideas.

Imagine, if you will, the dusty streets of ancient Jerusalem. The air is filled with the sounds of craftsmen at work, their tools clanging and scraping as they shape stone and metal. These artisans, though they might not have used the term, were the technologists of their day. Their craft was not just a means of making a living but a way of glorifying God through the work of their hands.

This connection between faith and human creativity is deeply rooted in Scripture. In the very first chapter of Genesis, we see God as the ultimate Creator, forming the universe and all that is in it. And then, in a moment of profound significance, God creates humanity in His own image. As it's written in Genesis 1:27, "So God created mankind in his own image, in the image of God he created them; male and female he created them."

This divine spark of creativity, this image of God within us, is the foundation for all human innovation, including what we now call technology. It's a reflection of our Creator's nature and forms part of our calling to be stewards of God's creation. As C.S. Lewis beautifully puts it in "Mere Christianity," "God is no fonder of intellectual slackers than of any other slackers. If you are thinking of becoming a Christian, I warn you, you are embarking on something which is going to take the whole of you, brains and all."

Throughout the Bible, we see examples of God-inspired innovation that we might consider technological advancements of their time. Consider

Noah's Ark, a massive engineering project guided by divine instruction. The detailed specifications God provided for its construction in Genesis 6-9 showcase not just divine wisdom but also an appreciation for human skill and craftsmanship.

Or think about the Tabernacle and later Solomon's Temple, described in exquisite detail in Exodus 25-31 and 1 Kings 6, respectively. These were not just places of worship, but marvels of architecture and artistry that required advanced knowledge of metallurgy, woodworking, and textile production. The craftsmen who created these sacred spaces were using the cutting-edge technology of their day to create a dwelling place for God's presence.

Even in times of national crisis, we see technology and faith intersecting. Nehemiah's rebuilding of Jerusalem's walls, recounted in Nehemiah 2-6, was as much a feat of engineering and project management as it was a act of spiritual restoration. Nehemiah had to coordinate resources, manage teams of workers, and implement defensive strategies – all while maintaining a spirit of prayer and dependence on God.

These biblical narratives remind us that the ability to create and innovate is part of our divine nature, reflecting the image of God in humanity. As the Apostle Paul reminds us in Ephesians 2:10, "For we are God's handiwork, created in Christ Jesus to do good works, which God prepared in advance for us to do." Our technological capabilities, then, can be seen as part of these good works prepared for us by God.

As we move beyond the biblical era, we see this interplay between faith and technology continuing to shape the development of both realms. The early Christian church, for instance, was quick to adopt and adapt the technologies of its time for the spread of the Gospel.

One of the most significant technological advancements that aided the spread of Christianity was the Roman road system. This marvel of ancient engineering, with its network of well-maintained roads spanning the empire, played a crucial role in the rapid dissemination of the Gospel. The Apostle Paul's missionary journeys, recounted in the Book of Acts, were made possible by these roads. In a sense, the Roman roads were the information superhighway of their day, allowing the message of Christ to travel faster and farther than ever before.

But it wasn't just transportation technology that aided the early church. The development of the codex – what we would recognize as the modern book format – was another technological innovation that had a profound impact on the spread of Christianity. The codex, with its bound pages, was more compact and easier to use than scrolls. Early Christians were among the first to widely adopt this new technology, using it to compile and distribute the Scriptures and other religious texts.

As we move into the medieval period, we see monasteries becoming centers of technological innovation. Monks were not just preservers of ancient knowledge, but also innovators in fields like agriculture, brewing, and timekeeping. The mechanical clock, for instance, was developed in medieval monasteries as a way to more accurately observe the canonical hours of prayer. This innovation would revolutionize how society as a whole measured and conceived of time.

But perhaps no technological advancement had a more profound impact on the intersection of faith and technology than the invention of the printing press by Johannes Gutenberg in the 15th century. This revolutionary technology allowed for the mass production of books, most notably the Bible. For the first time in history, the Word of God became accessible to a wide audience, no longer confined to handwritten manuscripts in monasteries.

The impact of the printing press on the spread of religious knowledge and the democratization of faith cannot be overstated. It aligned perfectly with the biblical mandate found in Matthew 28:19-20, "Therefore go and make disciples of all nations, baptizing them in the name of the Father and of the Son and of the Holy Spirit, and teaching them to obey everything I have commanded you." The printing press made it possible to 'go and make disciples' on a scale never before imagined.

Ravi Zacharias, in his book "Beyond Opinion," reflects on the impact of the printing press: "The Reformation's call to return to the authority of Scripture was made possible by the timely invention of the printing press. The Word of God was now accessible to the common person, no longer the sole property of the clergy or the educated elite."

The printing press also played a crucial role in the Protestant Reformation. Martin Luther's 95 Theses, which sparked the Reformation, spread rapidly throughout Europe thanks to the printing press. This technology allowed reformers to disseminate their ideas quickly and widely, challenging the established religious order and reshaping the Christian landscape.

As we move into the Renaissance and the Scientific Revolution, we see a new chapter in the relationship between faith and technology. Many of the pioneering scientists of this period were deeply religious individuals who saw their scientific pursuits as a way of understanding God's creation. For instance, Sir Isaac Newton, whose laws of motion and universal gravitation revolutionized our understanding of the physical world, was a devout Christian who wrote extensively on theology. He saw no conflict between his scientific work and his faith, famously stating, "This most beautiful system of the sun, planets, and comets, could only proceed from the counsel and dominion of an intelligent and powerful Being."

However, this period also saw the beginnings of tension between some religious institutions and scientific advancement. The trial of Galileo Galilei by the Roman Catholic Church in the 17th century is often cited as an example of this conflict. Yet, it's important to note that this tension was not universal across all faith traditions or even within the Catholic Church itself. Many religious thinkers and institutions continued to embrace scientific and technological progress as a means of better understanding and glorifying God's creation.

John Stott, in his book "Issues Facing Christians Today," offers a balanced perspective on this period: "The so-called conflict between science and religion is largely a myth... The real conflict is between two philosophies, not between science and faith. It is between the philosophy of materialism (that matter is all there is) and the philosophy of theism (that there is a Creator)."

The Industrial Revolution of the 18th and 19th centuries brought about unprecedented technological change, which had significant implications for religious life and practice. The rise of factories and urbanization changed the social fabric of many communities, challenging traditional religious structures and practices. At the same time, new technologies enabled the mass production of religious texts and artifacts, making them more widely available than ever before.

In response to these changes, many religious communities found innovative ways to incorporate new technologies into their practices. The use of the telegraph and, later, the telephone allowed for rapid communication between religious leaders and their congregations across vast distances. The development of railway systems facilitated pilgrimage and missionary work on an unprecedented scale.

As we reflect on this long history of the intersection between faith and technology, we can observe several consistent themes. First, innovation has often been in service of faith. Time and again, religious communities have embraced new technologies to enhance their practices, spread their message, and deepen their understanding of their faith.

Second, ethical considerations have always been at the forefront. As new technologies emerge, faith communities have often been at the forefront of considering their ethical implications, guided by their religious principles and values. This tradition of ethical reflection on technology continues to this day, particularly as we grapple with the implications of artificial intelligence and other emerging technologies.

Third, we see a pattern of adaptation and resilience in religious traditions in the face of technological change. While there have been moments of tension between faith and technology, there have also been numerous examples of reconciliation and integration. Religious communities have consistently found ways to maintain their core beliefs and practices while engaging with new technological realities.

Another significant theme is the democratization of knowledge. Technological advancements have often led to greater access to religious knowledge and practices, challenging traditional hierarchies and empowering individual believers. This aligns with the biblical principle found in Acts 17:11, which praises the Bereans, who "received the message with great eagerness and examined the Scriptures every day to see if what Paul said was true."

As we stand on the cusp of new technological frontiers, including artificial intelligence, virtual and augmented reality, and biotechnology, we find ourselves in a position not unlike our spiritual ancestors. Like them, we are called to engage thoughtfully and critically with new technologies, discerning how they can be used to enhance faith and serve humanity while remaining true to our core beliefs and values.

The words of the prophet Daniel seem particularly relevant as we consider the rapid pace of technological change in our time: "But you, Daniel, roll up and seal the words of the scroll until the time of the end. Many will go here and there to increase knowledge" (Daniel 12:4). In our rapidly advancing technological age, we are indeed seeing an unprecedented increase in knowledge and the resulting capabilities.

As we move forward in our exploration of artificial intelligence in ministry, may we carry with us the lessons of this rich history. May we approach new technologies with the same spirit of innovation, ethical reflection, and faithful adaptation that has characterized the intersection of faith and technology throughout the ages. May we always remember, as Timothy Keller puts it in his book "Every Good Endeavor," that "All work – be it in music, commerce, government, medicine, or any other field – is a way of participating in God's work of renewing and caring for the world."

In the next section, we'll delve deeper into the specific technological advancements that have shaped Christian practice in the modern era. As we do so, let us carry forward the understanding that our engagement with technology is not separate from our faith but an integral part of our calling to be salt and light in the world, using every tool at our disposal to glorify God and serve our fellow human beings.

Section 1.2: Technological Advancements in the Christian Community

As we step into the 20th century, we find ourselves on the brink of a technological revolution that would reshape the landscape of Christian ministry in ways our forebears could scarcely have imagined. The story of technology in the modern church is one of innovation, adaptation, and sometimes tension, as believers sought to harness new tools to spread the timeless message of the Gospel.

Imagine, if you will, a quiet Sunday evening in 1921. Families across America are gathered in their living rooms, huddled around a strange new device – the radio. Suddenly, the air is filled with the crackling voice of a preacher, bringing the word of God directly into their homes. This scene marks the beginning of a new era in Christian communication.

The advent of radio broadcasting opened up unprecedented possibilities for reaching the masses with the Christian message. In 1922, KFUO, in St. Louis, Missouri, became the first radio station owned and operated by a Christian denomination (the Lutheran Church-Missouri Synod). This pioneering effort paved the way for a new era of Christian broadcasting.

Radio evangelism quickly gained momentum. Programs like Charles E. Fuller's "Old Fashioned Revival Hour," which began in 1937, reached millions of listeners each week. These broadcasts not only spread the Gospel message but also provided comfort and spiritual guidance during challenging times such as the Great Depression and World War II.

The ability to reach people in their homes with the spoken word of Scripture and preaching represented a significant leap forward in the church's capacity to fulfill its mission. As A.W. Tozer, a pastor and author who lived through this period, noted, "It is scarcely possible in most places to get anyone to attend a meeting where the only attraction is God."

Radio changed this dynamic, bringing the attraction of God directly into people's homes. It allowed the church to reach those who might never darken the door of a physical church building, fulfilling in a new way Jesus' command to "go into all the world and preach the gospel to all creation" (Mark 16:15).

But the technological revolution was just beginning. As the mid-20th century approached, a new medium emerged that would captivate the world and provide yet another powerful tool for Christian ministry – television.

Picture a family in the 1960s gathered around their television set. The black-and-white screen flickers to life, and there, larger than life, is a charismatic preacher speaking with passion about the love of Christ. This was the dawn of televangelism, and it would forever change the face of Christian outreach.

In 1960, Pat Robertson founded the Christian Broadcasting Network (CBN), marking the beginning of a new era in Christian media. Programs like "The 700 Club" combined preaching with news and entertainment from a Christian perspective, reaching millions of viewers across the globe.

Television ministries also revolutionized fundraising and donor engagement within the Christian community. Telethons and direct appeals to viewers created new models for supporting Christian ministries, allowing them to engage supporters far beyond their local communities.

However, this expanded reach also brought challenges. The potential for financial mismanagement and the temptation to prioritize entertainment value over spiritual depth became real concerns. As John Stott wisely cautioned, "The Christian landscape is strewn with the wreckage of derelict, half-built towers—the ruins of those who began to build and were unable to finish. For thousands of people still ignore Christ's warning and undertake to follow him without first pausing to reflect on the cost of doing so."

The rise of cable and satellite television in the 1980s and 1990s led to the creation of dedicated Christian television networks, such as Trinity Broadcasting Network (TBN) and Daystar. These networks provided 24/7 Christian programming, further expanding the reach and influence of televised ministry.

But even as television was reshaping Christian outreach, another technological revolution was brewing – one that would have perhaps the most profound impact yet on how Christians engage with their faith and share it with others.

The late 20th century saw the emergence of the personal computer, a device that would soon become as common in homes as televisions. For the Christian community, this new technology opened up exciting possibilities for biblical study and ministry.

Imagine a pastor in the early 1990s, sitting at a bulky desktop computer. With a few clicks, he's able to access multiple Bible translations, cross-reference passages, and delve into original language texts – all tasks that would have required a small library and hours of manual searching just a few years earlier.

Bible software programs like Logos (founded in 1992) and BibleWorks (released in 1992) transformed biblical scholarship and personal Bible study. These programs allowed for complex searches, cross-referencing, and access to multiple translations and commentaries at the click of a button. The depth and breadth of study made possible by these tools have empowered both clergy and laity to engage with Scripture in new and profound ways.

As R.C. Sproul, a theologian who embraced these new tools, observed, "The only way to progress in the Christian life is through the study of the Word. It is impossible to use the sword of the Spirit, which is the Word of God, without a proper understanding of the sacred text."

But the digital revolution was just beginning. The advent of the internet in the 1990s marked the beginning of a new digital age for Christian ministry. Early Christian websites, such as Bible Gateway (launched in 1993), provided free online access to numerous Bible translations. Christian forums and chat rooms allowed believers from around the world to connect, discuss their faith, and support one another. This global connectivity facilitated cross-cultural understanding and cooperation among Christians from diverse backgrounds.

As internet technology advanced, so did its applications in Christian ministry. Online streaming capabilities allowed churches to broadcast their services live over the internet, reaching audiences far beyond their physical locations. Podcasting, which gained popularity in the early 2000s, provided a new platform for distributing sermons, Bible studies, and Christian teaching.

The rise of social media platforms in the early 21st century further transformed how Christians connect and share their faith. Facebook, launched in 2004, and Twitter, founded in 2006, became powerful tools for sharing inspirational messages, promoting events, and engaging with both believers and non-believers. Many pastors and Christian leaders have built significant online followings, allowing them to reach far beyond their local congregations.

Timothy Keller, a pastor who has effectively used social media to extend his ministry, notes, "Social media is a tool, and like any tool, it can be used for good or ill. Our challenge is to use it in a way that glorifies God and serves others."

Instagram, introduced in 2010, added a visual dimension to social media ministry, with many churches and Christian influencers using the platform to share inspirational images and short video messages. The launch of TikTok in 2016 (globally in 2018) opened up new possibilities for short-form video content, with many Christian content creators using the platform to reach younger audiences with bite-sized spiritual messages.

The proliferation of smartphones in the late 2000s and early 2010s brought about another significant shift in how Christians engage with their faith. Mobile apps made it possible to access spiritual resources anytime, anywhere. The YouVersion Bible app, launched in 2008, has been downloaded over 500 million times and offers hundreds of Bible translations and reading plans. Other popular Christian apps include prayer reminders, daily devotionals, and Christian music streaming services.

This constant access to spiritual resources has transformed personal devotion and Bible study. As John Piper observes, "When a person is born of God and they have the Bible in front of them, they are not just reading the words of a book. The light of God's glory is shining into their hearts."

Cloud computing technology has also had a significant impact on church administration and community management. Church management software (ChMS) like Planning Center (launched in 2006) and Faithlife Equip (introduced in 2020) have streamlined administrative tasks, member communication, and resource allocation for churches of all sizes.

The COVID-19 pandemic in 2020 accelerated the adoption of digital technologies in Christian communities. With in-person gatherings restricted, churches quickly pivoted to online services, utilizing platforms like Zoom, YouTube, and Facebook Live. This shift demonstrated the resilience and adaptability of Christian communities in the face of challenges. It also highlighted the potential of digital technologies to maintain and even strengthen faith communities during times of physical separation.

As we look to the future, emerging technologies open new frontiers for Christian ministry. Virtual and Augmented Reality (VR/AR) technologies are beginning to find applications in Christian contexts. Some churches and ministries are experimenting with VR church services, allowing people to attend and interact in virtual environments. For example, DJ Soto's VR Church, launched in 2016, conducts services entirely in virtual reality.

AR apps have been developed to enhance Bible study, overlaying additional information or visualizations onto physical Bibles or religious sites. Imagine opening your Bible and seeing the lands of Israel come to life before your eyes or visiting a historic church and being able to see and hear the great preachers of the past deliver their most famous sermons.

Artificial Intelligence (AI) and machine learning technologies are also starting to impact the Christian community. AI-powered chatbots are being used for basic pastoral care and to answer common questions about faith. Some organizations are exploring the use of AI for Bible translation, potentially accelerating the process of making Scripture available in every language.

Blockchain technology, while still in its early stages of adoption in Christian circles, has the potential to increase transparency in church finances and facilitate secure, borderless donations for mission work. Some ministries are also exploring the use of non-fungible tokens (NFTs) for fundraising and community building.

The integration of Internet of Things (IoT) devices in church buildings is another emerging trend. Smart systems for lighting, heating, and security can improve energy efficiency and enhance the worship experience. Some churches are using IoT sensors to track attendance and engagement, providing valuable data for ministry planning.

As we survey this technological advancement landscape in the Christian community, we're reminded of G.K. Chesterton's words: "The Christian ideal has not been tried and found wanting. It has been found difficult and left untried." In many ways, these new technologies are allowing us to try—to live out and share our faith—in ways that were previously impossible.

Yet, as we embrace these new tools, we must also grapple with their challenges. The church must address issues of digital addiction, the erosion of face-to-face community, and the potential for technology to distract from rather than enhance spiritual growth.

Moreover, as we leverage technology for ministry, we must be mindful of the digital divide – the gap between those who have access to technology and those who do not. How can we ensure that our embrace of technology doesn't inadvertently exclude or marginalize certain members of our communities?

As we move forward into this brave new world of technology-enhanced ministry, may we do so with wisdom and discernment. May we harness these powerful tools to spread the unchanging message of God's love, always remembering that our ultimate reliance is not on technology but on the power of the Holy Spirit.

In the next chapter, we'll begin to explore the specific ways in which artificial intelligence is being used in ministry today. As we do so, let us carry forward the lessons of history – both the opportunities and the challenges that new technologies present. And let us always keep in mind the words of the Apostle Paul in 1 Corinthians 9:22-23: "I have become all things to all people so that by all possible means I might save some. I do all this for the sake of the gospel, that I may share in its blessings."

Section 1.3: Embracing Technology in Ministry

The rapid pace of technological advancement presents both opportunities and challenges for modern ministry. As we explore how to embrace technology in ministry, it's crucial to approach this integration with wisdom, discernment, and a clear understanding of our core mission as followers of Christ.

The Apostle Paul's words in 1 Corinthians 9:22-23 provide a foundational principle for considering the use of technology in ministry: "To the weak I became weak, to win the weak. I have become all things to all people so that by all possible means I might save some. I do all this for the sake of the gospel, that I may share in its blessings." This passage emphasizes the importance of adaptability in ministry, of using all available means to reach people with the message of Christ. In our contemporary context, technology represents one of these means.

One of the primary reasons for embracing technology in ministry is its potential to amplify our reach and effectiveness in spreading the Gospel. Social media platforms, for instance, allow churches and individual believers to share the message of Christ with a global audience. A single post can reach thousands, if not millions, of people across geographical and cultural boundaries. Live streaming services enable churches to minister to those who cannot physically attend, whether due to illness, distance, or other constraints.

However, as we leverage these technologies, we must be mindful of the warning in Mark 8:36: "What good is it for someone to gain the whole world, yet forfeit their soul?" While technology can expand our reach, we must ensure that our use of these tools doesn't compromise the depth and authenticity of our message or our relationships.

In the realm of discipleship and spiritual formation, technology offers powerful tools for enhancing Bible study and personal devotion. Bible apps and digital study tools have made it easier than ever for believers to engage with Scripture daily. Features like verse of the day, reading plans, and multiple translations at one's fingertips encourage regular Bible reading and study. This aligns with the exhortation in 2 Timothy 2:15: "Do your best to present yourself to God as one approved, a worker who does not need to be ashamed and who correctly handles the word of truth."

However, it's important to note that while these tools can facilitate Bible study, they cannot replace the work of the Holy Spirit in illuminating Scripture and transforming lives. As Jesus said in John 14:26, "But the Advocate, the Holy Spirit, whom the Father will send in my name, will teach you all things and will remind you of everything I have said to you." Technology can provide access to information, but true understanding and application come through the work of the Holy Spirit in the believer's life.

Artificial Intelligence (AI) is increasingly being used in various aspects of ministry, from chatbots answering basic faith questions to algorithms suggesting personalized devotional content. While these can be valuable tools, it's crucial to understand that AI is meant to assist us in our walk with Christ, not to replace the guidance and work of the Holy Spirit or human pastoral care.

AI can process vast amounts of information and provide insights, but it lacks the divine wisdom and personal relationships that are central to the Christian faith. As Proverbs 3:5-6 reminds us, "Trust in the Lord with all your heart and lean not on your own understanding; in all your ways submit to him, and he will make your paths straight." While we can use AI as a tool, our ultimate trust and guidance must come from God.

In embracing technology for ministry, we must also be mindful of the digital divide. Not everyone has equal access to technology, and as we incorporate these tools into our ministry, we must ensure that we're not inadvertently excluding those who lack access to technological literacy. This aligns with the biblical principle of caring for the marginalized, as exemplified in James 2:1-4, which warns against showing favoritism.

To address this issue, some churches have implemented digital literacy programs for their congregations, particularly targeting older members or those from disadvantaged backgrounds. Others have partnered with local organizations to provide internet access and devices to those in need. These efforts not only bridge the digital divide but also demonstrate the church's commitment to inclusivity and community service.

Another crucial consideration in embracing technology for ministry is the need for digital discipleship. As more of our lives and our ministries move online, we must learn to apply biblical principles to our digital interactions. This includes practicing integrity, kindness, and wisdom in our online communications. Ephesians 4:29 provides a good guideline: "Do not let any unwholesome talk come out of your mouths, but only what is helpful for building others up according to their needs, that it may benefit those who listen." This principle applies equally to our digital "speech."

Digital discipleship also involves teaching believers how to navigate the online world in a way that honors God and reflects Christian values. This might include discussions on social media etiquette, how to respond to online conflicts in a Christ-like manner, and how to discern truth from misinformation online. Some churches have developed specific curricula or small group studies focused on these topics.

Embracing technology in ministry also means being good stewards of these tools. This involves not only using them effectively but also being aware of their potential pitfalls. For instance, the addictive nature of some technologies can distract us from our spiritual lives if not managed wisely. As Paul writes in 1 Corinthians 6:12, "'I have the right to do anything,' you say—but not everything is beneficial. 'I have the right to do anything'—but I will not be mastered by anything." We must ensure that our use of technology serves our ministry and doesn't become a hindrance to our spiritual growth.

To this end, some Christian leaders have advocated for regular "digital fasts" or "tech Sabbaths," encouraging believers to periodically unplug from technology to focus on prayer, reflection, and face-to-face relationships. Others have developed resources to help believers practice "mindful" or intentional use of technology, aligning their digital habits with their spiritual values.

The use of technology in worship is another area that requires careful consideration. While multimedia presentations, online giving platforms, and sophisticated sound systems can enhance the worship experience, we must be cautious not to let the medium overshadow the message. Jesus' words in John 4:24 remind us of the essence of true worship: "God is spirit, and his worshipers must worship in the Spirit and in truth." Technology should facilitate, not dominate, our worship.

Some churches have found creative ways to use technology to enhance worship while maintaining its spiritual focus. For example, some use projection systems to display multilingual lyrics, making services more accessible to diverse congregations. Others use social media to encourage real-time prayer requests or testimonies during services, fostering a sense of community participation.

As we embrace technology in ministry, we must also be prepared to address the theological and ethical questions that arise from new technologies. Issues such as artificial intelligence, genetic engineering, and virtual reality raise profound questions about the nature of humanity, consciousness, and our relationship with God. Christian leaders and thinkers need to engage with these issues, providing biblical perspectives and guidance.

This engagement might take the form of a sermon series addressing the ethical implications of new technologies, small group studies exploring the intersection of faith and science, or the development of position papers or guidelines for the ethical use of technology in ministry contexts. Some seminaries and Christian universities have even begun offering courses or degree programs focusing on theology and technology.

The rapid pace of technological change can be overwhelming, but we can find encouragement in the words of Isaiah 40:31: "but those who hope in the Lord will renew their strength. They will soar on wings like eagles; they will run and not grow weary, they will walk and not be faint." Our strength and guidance ultimately come from God, not from technology.

Embracing technology in ministry also means being willing to learn and adapt. This can be challenging, especially for those who are not naturally inclined towards technology. However, the biblical principle of stewardship calls us to make the best use of the resources available to us. As the Parable of the Talents

67

in Matthew 25:14-30 teaches us, we are called to use and multiply the gifts we've been given, which in our modern context includes technological tools.

Many churches have responded to this challenge by offering technology training for staff and volunteers, ensuring that those involved in ministry are equipped to use the tools available to them effectively. Some have created "tech ministries," teams of technologically savvy members who support the church's digital efforts and help train others.

It's also important to maintain a balance between innovation and tradition in ministry. While we embrace new technologies, we shouldn't discard the time-tested practices that have nurtured faith for generations. As Jesus said in Matthew 13:52, "Therefore every teacher of the law who has become a disciple in the kingdom of heaven is like the owner of a house who brings out of his storeroom new treasures as well as old." We should seek to integrate new technologies with traditional practices in ways that enrich our faith and ministry.

This integration might involve using digital tools to enhance traditional practices rather than replace them. For example, some churches have created apps that complement their physical prayer journals, allowing believers to record and track their prayers digitally while maintaining the practice of regular, intentional prayer. Others have used virtual reality to create immersive Bible study experiences that bring ancient biblical settings to life, enhancing rather than replacing traditional Scripture study.

As we look to the future, emerging technologies like advanced AI, virtual and augmented reality, and biotechnology will likely present new opportunities and challenges for the ministry. As Christian leaders and communities, we must stay informed about these developments and prayerfully discern how to engage with them in ways that honor God and serve His people.

For instance, as AI continues to advance, we may need to grapple with questions about the nature of consciousness and the ethical implications of creating machines that can think and reason. Virtual and augmented reality technologies may offer new ways to create immersive worship experiences or to reach those who are physically isolated, but we'll need to consider how to maintain genuine community and embodied faith in an increasingly virtual world.

In all of this, we must remember that while technology can enhance our ministry efforts, it is not the source of our power or effectiveness. As Paul reminds us in 1 Corinthians 2:4-5, "My message and my preaching were not with wise and persuasive words, but with a demonstration of the Spirit's power, so that your faith might not rest on human wisdom, but on God's power." Our ultimate reliance must always be on God's power working through us, not on our technological capabilities.

This principle should guide our approach to technology in ministry. We should view technological tools as a means to an end, not ends in themselves. The goal is not to have the most advanced technology or the most impressive online presence but to use these tools effectively to share the love of Christ, make disciples, and build up the body of believers.

As we embrace technology in ministry, we must also be mindful of the potential for technology to create barriers or reinforce existing inequalities. The Apostle James warns against showing favoritism in the church (James 2:1-13), and this principle should extend to our use of technology. We must strive to ensure that our technological initiatives are inclusive and accessible to all members of our community, regardless of their economic status, age, or technological literacy.

This might involve providing training and support for those less comfortable with technology, ensuring that traditional, non-technological means of engagement remain available, or even working to address broader issues of digital access in our communities. Some churches have partnered with local organizations to provide internet access or devices to underserved areas, seeing this as an extension of their ministry and outreach efforts.

Privacy and data security are also crucial considerations as we embrace technology in ministry. As stewards of our congregants' personal information, we have a responsibility to protect their privacy and use their data ethically. This aligns with the biblical principle of trustworthiness, as exemplified in 1 Corinthians 4:2: "Now it is required that those who have been given a trust must prove faithful."

Practically, this might involve implementing robust data protection measures, being transparent about how data is collected and used, and ensuring that any third-party tools or services we use adhere to high standards of privacy and security. It also means being thoughtful about what data we collect and why, always prioritizing the well-being and trust of our community members over the potential insights or efficiencies that more data might provide.

As we navigate the complex landscape of technology in ministry, it's crucial to foster ongoing dialogue and discernment within our faith communities. This might involve creating forums for discussing the implications of new technologies, encouraging critical thinking about the role of technology in our spiritual lives, and regularly reassessing our technological initiatives in light of our core values and mission.

Some churches have found it helpful to establish technology committees or task forces to guide their digital strategies and ensure that technological decisions align with the church's overall mission and values. Others have integrated discussions of technology and faith into their regular teaching and discipleship programs, recognizing that digital literacy and discernment are increasingly important aspects of Christian formation in the 21st century.

It's also important to remember that embracing technology in ministry is not just about adopting new tools but about cultivating a mindset of innovation and adaptability. This doesn't mean chasing after every new trend but rather being open to new ways of fulfilling our timeless mission. As Paul adapted his ministry approach to different cultural contexts (1 Corinthians 9:19-23), we too must be willing to adapt our methods to effectively reach and serve people in our digital age.

This adaptive mindset should be balanced with a strong grounding in our core beliefs and values. As we experiment with new technologies and approaches, we must always evaluate them against the teachings of Scripture and the traditions of our faith. The goal is not innovation for its own sake but innovation in service of more effectively sharing the unchanging message of the Gospel.

In conclusion, embracing technology in ministry is about leveraging these tools to fulfill our calling as followers of Christ more effectively. It's about using every means at our disposal to share the unchanging message of God's love and redemption. As we navigate this digital age, may we do so with wisdom, discernment, and an unwavering commitment to the truth of the Gospel.

Let us use technology as a tool to amplify our witness, deepen our faith, and extend the reach of God's kingdom, always remembering that our true power comes not from our technological prowess but from the indwelling presence of the Holy Spirit. As we move forward in this digital age, may our use of technology in ministry always be guided by Paul's exhortation in Colossians 3:17: "And whatever you do, whether in word or deed, do it all in the name of the Lord Jesus, giving thanks to God the Father through him."

CHAPTER TWO

Why AI in the Ministry?

Section 2.1: The Relevance of AI in Modern Ministry

In an era where technology permeates every aspect of our lives, the church finds itself at a critical juncture. As pastors and ministry leaders, we are called to be faithful stewards of the resources God has entrusted to us, including the technological advancements of our time. Artificial Intelligence (AI) stands at the forefront of these advancements, offering unprecedented opportunities to enhance and extend our ministry efforts. But why should we, as servants of God, consider incorporating AI into our work?

The relevance of AI in modern ministry stems from its unique ability to process and analyze vast amounts of data, recognize complex patterns, and generate insights that can inform and enhance our service to God and our communities. Unlike previous technologies that primarily facilitated communication or information access, AI has the potential to augment decision-making processes, personalize spiritual experiences, and even assist in tasks that were once thought to be exclusively human domains.

As C.S. Lewis wisely noted, "God is no fonder of intellectual slackers than of any other slackers. If you are thinking of becoming a Christian, I warn you, you are embarking on something which is going to take the whole of you, brains and all." This sentiment applies not just to our personal faith journey but also to how we approach ministry in an ever-changing world. Engaging with AI is, in many ways, a continuation of this tradition of intellectual engagement and adaptive ministry.

One of the primary reasons to consider AI in ministry is its potential to amplify our efforts in sharing God's love and building His kingdom. In an increasingly digital and data-driven world, AI can help us reach people where they are, personalizing our outreach and making our ministries more effective and efficient. Consider the parable of the sower in

Matthew 13. Jesus tells of a farmer scattering seed, which falls on different types of soil with varying results. In our modern context, AI could be seen as a tool to help us identify the "good soil" – those most receptive to the Gospel message – and tailor our approach to effectively plant the seeds of faith.

For instance, AI-powered analytics can help us understand patterns in church attendance, engagement with online content, and community needs. This information can guide our outreach strategies, helping us to more effectively allocate resources and tailor our messages to resonate with different segments of our congregation and community. As stewards of God's resources, we have a responsibility to use every tool at our disposal to maximize the impact of our ministry efforts.

Another compelling reason to explore AI in ministry is its potential to free up time and resources for more relational and spiritual aspects of church life. Many pastors and ministry leaders find themselves bogged down in administrative tasks, leaving less time for prayer, study, and personal interaction with their congregation. AI could help streamline these administrative duties, allowing church leaders to focus more on their core calling.

Imagine a church management system powered by AI that could automatically schedule rooms for various ministries, predict attendance trends for different services or events, and even suggest budgeting strategies based on historical data and ministry goals. Such a system could save countless hours of administrative work, allowing pastors and ministry leaders to invest more time in prayer, sermon preparation, and personal ministry.

In the realm of pastoral care, AI offers powerful tools to enhance our ability to shepherd our flocks. While AI can never replace the personal touch and spiritual discernment of a pastor, it can serve as a valuable support tool. For example, AI systems can help identify patterns in congregational needs, flagging potential crisis situations that may require immediate pastoral attention.

An AI system might notice that a usually active member has been absent from both physical and online church activities for several weeks. Simultaneously, it might detect an increase in searches for topics related to grief or depression on the church's website from an account associated with this member. By correlating this information, the system could alert pastoral staff to reach out, potentially providing timely support during a difficult period in the member's life.

Moreover, AI can assist in identifying broader trends within the congregation. By analyzing aggregate data on engagement with different ministries, sermon topics, or small group activities, AI can provide insights into the spiritual health and interests of the church community as a whole. This information can be invaluable for church leaders in tailoring their teaching and ministry focus to address the most pressing needs and interests of their congregation.

In the area of Bible study and sermon preparation, AI offers tools that can significantly enhance the depth and breadth of our engagement with Scripture. AI-powered research assistants can quickly analyze vast libraries of theological works, commentaries, and historical documents, providing relevant insights and connections that might take a human researcher weeks or months to uncover.

For example, a pastor preparing a sermon on a specific Bible passage could use an AI research tool to instantly access relevant cross-references, historical context, original language insights, and even contemporary application ideas. The AI could also suggest relevant illustrations or current events that connect with the themes of the passage. This doesn't replace the need for personal study and Spirit-led interpretation, but it can certainly enrich our understanding and application of God's Word.

As John Stott reminds us, "Knowledge is indispensable to Christian life and service. If we do not use the mind which God has given us, we condemn ourselves to spiritual superficiality." AI can be a powerful tool in our pursuit of deeper knowledge and understanding of God's Word, helping us to more effectively teach and apply Scripture in our ministries.

In the realm of evangelism and outreach, AI's relevance becomes even more apparent. Traditional methods of community analysis and outreach planning often rely on limited data sets and human intuition. While these remain valuable, AI can significantly enhance these efforts by analyzing vast amounts of demographic data, social media trends, and community needs. This can help churches identify underserved populations, understand the changing dynamics of their local communities, and tailor their outreach strategies for maximum impact.

For example, an AI system might analyze local demographic data, social media conversations, and community forum discussions to identify emerging needs or interests in the area surrounding a church. It might detect an influx of young families into the neighborhood, an increase in discussions about work-life balance, or growing concern about mental health issues among teenagers. Armed with these insights, church leaders can develop targeted outreach programs, adjust their messaging, or even consider new ministry initiatives that directly address these community needs.

Furthermore, AI can assist in optimizing the timing and channels for outreach efforts. By analyzing patterns of online engagement and community activity, AI can suggest the most effective times to host events, send communications, or launch new initiatives. This level of data-driven decision-making was previously impossible at scale and offers new opportunities for churches to be more strategic and effective in their community engagement efforts.

In the context of global missions, AI's relevance is underscored by its potential to assist in language translation and cultural understanding. As AI-powered translation tools become more sophisticated, they can facilitate real-time cross-cultural communication, breaking down language barriers that have traditionally been major challenges in mission work. This technology could enable missionaries to communicate more effectively in new cultural contexts, even before they've fully mastered the local language.

Moreover, AI can assist in the contextualization of the Gospel message for different cultural settings. By analyzing cultural data, local customs, and linguistic nuances, AI can provide insights that help missionaries and church planters present the unchanging truth of the Gospel in ways that resonate with local cultures. This aligns with the Great Commission's call to make disciples of all nations, leveraging technology to overcome linguistic and cultural barriers.

However, as we consider the relevance of AI in ministry, we must also be mindful of the potential challenges and ethical considerations it presents. As Timothy Keller wisely cautions, "Truth without love is imperious self-righteousness. Love without truth is cowardly self-indulgence." While AI can provide valuable data and insights, it cannot replace the compassion, discernment, and Spirit-led wisdom that are essential to effective ministry.

We must be cautious not to become overly reliant on technology, potentially neglecting the human and spiritual elements that are at the heart of Christian ministry. There's a risk of reducing complex spiritual and relational dynamics to mere data points or of prioritizing efficiency over genuine connection and spiritual growth.

Moreover, the use of AI in ministry raises important ethical questions about data privacy, algorithmic bias, and the appropriate boundaries of technology use in spiritual matters. As church leaders, we have a responsibility to engage thoughtfully with these issues, ensuring that our use of AI aligns with biblical principles of justice, compassion, and human dignity.

Despite these challenges, the potential benefits of AI in ministry are too significant to ignore. As A.W. Tozer once said, "It is not what a man does that determines whether his work is sacred or secular, it is why he does it." If our motivation in adopting AI is to fulfill our calling to love God and serve others more effectively, then its use can indeed be a sacred endeavor.

As we move forward in exploring the relevance of AI in ministry, let us do so with wisdom and discernment. Let us approach this new frontier with the mindset described by Jesus in Matthew 10:16, being "as shrewd as snakes and as innocent as doves." We must be willing to embrace new tools and methods, while always remaining grounded in the unchanging truth of the Gospel.

In the sections that follow, we'll delve deeper into the specific benefits AI can bring to various aspects of ministry work, and we'll examine real-world case studies of how churches and Christian organizations are already leveraging this technology to enhance their mission and outreach. As we embark on this journey, may we keep in mind the words of the Apostle Paul in 1 Corinthians 9:22-23: "I have become all things to all people so that by all possible means I might save some. I do all this for the sake of the gospel, that I may share in its blessings."

AI represents a powerful new "means" by which we can minister effectively in our increasingly digital world. As we explore its potential, may we do so with a spirit of innovation and faithfulness, always seeking to use these new tools in ways that honor God and serve His people. Let us approach this exploration with open minds and discerning hearts, remembering that our ultimate goal is not technological sophistication but faithfulness to our calling to love God, serve others, and make disciples of all nations.

Section 2.2: Benefits of AI in Enhancing Ministry Work

As we explore the benefits of AI in enhancing ministry work, it's important to approach this topic with both excitement for the possibilities and a grounded understanding of our core mission. The apostle Paul reminds us in 1 Corinthians 9:22-23, "I have become all things to all people so that by all possible means I might save some. I do all this for the sake of the gospel, that I may share in its blessings." In our modern context, AI represents a new "means" by which we can more effectively share the gospel and serve our communities.

One of the most significant benefits of AI in ministry is its ability to provide deep, actionable insights from vast amounts of data. In the context of a church or ministry organization, this data might include attendance records, giving patterns, ministry participation, online engagement metrics, and even unstructured data from sermon notes or prayer requests. AI's capacity to analyze this information and identify meaningful patterns can lead to more informed decision-making and strategic planning.

This benefit aligns with the biblical principle of wisdom in leadership. As Proverbs 24:3-4 tells us, "By wisdom a house is built, and through understanding it is established; through knowledge its rooms are filled with rare and beautiful treasures." AI can help ministry leaders gain a deeper understanding of their congregation and community, enabling them to make wiser decisions about resource allocation, program development, and outreach strategies.

Another substantial benefit of AI in ministry is its ability to personalize spiritual growth resources at scale. Traditional approaches to discipleship often rely on standardized curricula or programs, which may not resonate equally with all participants. AI can tailor spiritual growth plans to individual needs, learning styles, and interests.

This personalization aligns with the biblical concept of individual spiritual growth and the recognition that each believer is on a unique journey. As Paul writes in Philippians 2:12-13, "Therefore, my dear friends, as you have always obeyed—not only in my presence, but now much more in my absence—continue to work out your salvation with fear and trembling, for it is God who works in you to will and to act in order to fulfill his good purpose." AI can assist in this "working out" of salvation by providing personalized resources and guidance.

In the realm of pastoral care, AI offers several benefits that can enhance the work of ministry leaders. While AI cannot replace the personal touch and spiritual discernment of a pastor, it can serve as a valuable support tool. For example, AI-powered systems can help identify patterns in congregational needs, flagging potential crisis situations that may require immediate pastoral attention.

This aligns with the biblical mandate for shepherding the flock. As Peter instructs in 1 Peter 5:2-3, "Be shepherds of God's flock that is under your care, watching over them—not because you must, but because you are willing, as God wants you to be; not pursuing dishonest gain, but eager to serve; not lording it over those entrusted to you, but being examples to the flock." AI can help pastors be more proactive and comprehensive in their care, ensuring that fewer people fall through the cracks.

In the area of church administration, AI offers numerous benefits that can streamline operations and improve efficiency. Automating routine tasks such as scheduling, basic correspondence, and data entry frees up staff time for more relational and strategic work. AI can also enhance financial management by identifying spending patterns, predicting future giving trends, and even detecting potential fraudulent activity.

This efficiency in administration aligns with the biblical principle of good stewardship. Jesus' parable of the talents in Matthew 25:14-30 teaches us to be wise and productive with the resources entrusted to us. By leveraging AI to handle routine tasks more efficiently, churches can dedicate more of their human resources to direct ministry and outreach.

AI also offers significant benefits in the area of community outreach and evangelism. By analyzing demographic data, social media trends, and community information, AI can help churches identify underserved populations or emerging needs in their local area. This data-driven approach to community analysis can inform more targeted and effective outreach strategies.

This benefit aligns with Jesus' command in Matthew 28:19-20, "Therefore go and make disciples of all nations, baptizing them in the name of the Father and of the Son and of the Holy Spirit, and teaching them to obey everything I have commanded you." AI can help churches be more strategic and effective in their efforts to reach their communities with the gospel.

In the context of global missions, AI's language processing capabilities offer tremendous benefits. Real-time translation tools can facilitate communication between missionaries and local populations, breaking down language barriers that have traditionally been major challenges in cross-cultural ministry. AI can also assist in the complex task of Bible translation, potentially accelerating the process of making Scripture available in every language.

This benefit directly supports the fulfillment of the Great Commission. As Revelation 7:9 envisions, "After this I looked, and there before me was a great multitude that no one could count, from every nation, tribe, people and language, standing before the throne and before the Lamb." AI can help overcome language barriers that have historically hindered the spread of the gospel to all peoples.

In the realm of worship and music ministry, AI offers several benefits that can enhance creativity and efficiency. AI-powered music composition tools can assist worship leaders in creating new songs or arranging existing ones to fit their congregation's needs. These tools can suggest chord progressions, melodies, or even entire song structures based on input parameters such as mood, theme, or musical style.

While the core of worship will always be a heartfelt response to God, these AI tools can help worship leaders express that response in fresh and engaging ways. As Psalm 96:1 encourages, "Sing to the Lord a new song; sing to the Lord, all the earth." AI can assist in the creation of these "new songs," helping to keep worship vibrant and relevant.

For churches that produce audio or video content, AI offers significant benefits in post-production. AI-powered editing tools can automatically clean up audio, remove background noise, and even suggest optimal cuts for video content. This can greatly reduce the time and technical expertise required to produce high-quality media content, allowing churches to more effectively share their message through various media channels.

In the area of biblical research and sermon preparation, AI offers powerful tools that can enhance the depth and breadth of study. AI-powered research assistants can quickly analyze vast libraries of theological works, commentaries, and historical documents, providing relevant insights and connections that might take a human researcher weeks or months to uncover.

This benefit aligns with Paul's instruction to Timothy in 2 Timothy 2:15, "Do your best to present yourself to God as one approved, a worker who does not need to be ashamed and who correctly handles the word of truth." AI can assist preachers and teachers in more thoroughly and accurately handling Scripture, leading to richer, more insightful teaching.

In the realm of church security and child protection, AI offers significant benefits. Facial recognition systems can enhance security measures during church gatherings, alerting security personnel to the presence of known threats. AI-powered background check systems can assist in vetting volunteers, especially those working with children and vulnerable populations, by quickly analyzing vast amounts of public records and identifying potential red flags.

This use of AI aligns with the biblical mandate to protect the vulnerable. As James 1:27 instructs,

"Religion that God our Father accepts as pure and faultless is this: to look after orphans and widows in their distress and to keep oneself from being polluted by the world." By enhancing security measures, AI can help churches create safer environments for all, especially the most vulnerable.

Another area where AI offers substantial benefits is in fostering interfaith dialogue and understanding. AI-powered research tools can provide quick, comprehensive overviews of different faith traditions, helping Christian leaders engage more knowledgeably and respectfully with people of other beliefs. This can be particularly valuable in increasingly diverse communities where churches may be seeking to build bridges with other faith groups.

In the realm of apologetics and defending the faith, AI offers powerful tools for engaging with complex philosophical and scientific questions. AI research assistants can quickly compile relevant arguments, counter-arguments, and evidence from a wide range of sources, helping Christian thinkers and leaders respond more effectively to challenges to the faith.

This benefit supports the biblical call to "always be prepared to give an answer to everyone who asks you to give the reason for the hope that you have" (1 Peter 3:15). AI can help apologists and Christian thinkers be better prepared to engage with challenging questions and diverse worldviews.

For youth ministry, AI offers benefits in terms of engagement and relevance. AI-powered content recommendation systems can suggest age-appropriate resources, activities, and discussion topics that resonate with the current interests and challenges of young people. This can help youth leaders stay current and relatable in their ministry approach.

In terms of church growth and member assimilation, AI can provide valuable insights and automation. AI systems can analyze patterns of visitor engagement, identifying the most effective pathways for turning first-time guests into active members. They can automate follow-up processes, ensuring that new visitors receive personalized communications and invitations to relevant church events or small groups.

For larger churches or multi-site churches, AI can help maintain a sense of personalized ministry at scale. By analyzing individual members' involvement, interests, and needs, AI can help church leaders provide more targeted care and opportunities for involvement, even as the congregation grows beyond the point where leaders can personally know every member.

In the area of social justice and community service, AI can help churches more effectively identify and respond to needs in their communities. By analyzing public data on poverty rates, health outcomes, education levels, and other social indicators, AI can help churches target their outreach and service efforts for maximum impact.

This benefit aligns with the biblical mandate to seek justice and care for the poor. As Micah 6:8 instructs, "He has shown you, O mortal, what is good. And what does the Lord require of you? To act justly and to love mercy and to walk humbly with your God." AI can help churches more effectively fulfill this calling by providing data-driven insights into community needs.

For churches engaged in media ministry, such as producing podcasts, videos, or online courses, AI offers numerous benefits. From automated transcription and captioning to content recommendation systems that suggest relevant content to viewers, AI can enhance both the production and distribution of media content.

Finally, in the realm of prayer ministry, AI can provide support tools that enhance, rather than replace, human-led prayer. For instance, AI could analyze prayer requests to identify trends or urgent needs, helping prayer teams focus their efforts. It could also suggest relevant Scripture passages or prayer points based on the specific needs being addressed.

As we consider these myriad benefits of AI in ministry, it's crucial to remember that they are tools to enhance, not replace, the fundamentally relational and spiritual nature of Christian ministry. As Timothy Keller often reminds us, "Truth without love is imperious self-righteousness. Love without truth is cowardly self-indulgence." AI can provide valuable data, insights, and efficiency, but it cannot replace the love, compassion, and spiritual discernment that are at the heart of Christian ministry.

In conclusion, the benefits of AI in enhancing ministry work are vast and varied. From providing deep insights for strategic decision-making to personalizing spiritual growth resources, from streamlining administrative tasks to enhancing outreach efforts, AI offers powerful tools that can amplify the impact of ministry in the digital age.

However, it's crucial to remember that these benefits are realized not through blind adoption of technology, but through thoughtful, prayerful integration of AI tools in ways that align with the church's mission and values. As we harness these benefits, we must always keep in mind that AI is a tool to enhance, not replace, the fundamentally relational and spiritual nature of Christian ministry.

The ultimate goal in leveraging these benefits is not technological advancement for its own sake but more effective fulfillment of our calling to love God, serve others, and make disciples. As we embrace the benefits of AI in ministry, may we do so with wisdom, discernment, and an unwavering commitment to the timeless truths of our faith.

In the next section, we'll explore specific case studies of how churches and Christian organizations are implementing AI in their ministries, providing concrete examples of these benefits in action. As we do so, may we be inspired to consider how we might leverage these powerful tools in our own ministry contexts, always for the glory of God and the advancement of His Kingdom.

Section 2.3: Case Studies of AI in Ministry

As we explore the practical applications of AI in ministry, it's valuable to examine real-world examples of how churches and Christian organizations are leveraging this technology. These case studies offer concrete insights into the benefits, challenges, and lessons learned from implementing AI in various ministry contexts. As we consider these examples, let's keep in mind the words of the Apostle Paul in 1 Corinthians 10:23, "'I have the right to do anything,' you say—but not everything is beneficial. 'I have the right to do anything'—but not everything is constructive." This principle should guide our approach to AI in ministry, always evaluating whether its use truly serves our mission and glorifies God.

Case Study 1: AI-Enhanced Pastoral Care at First
Baptist Church of Austin, Texas

First Baptist Church of Austin, a congregation of over
5,000 members, implemented an AI-powered pastoral
care system they named "CareAssist" to support their
ministry team in providing comprehensive care for all
members.

CareAssist analyzes data from various sources,
including attendance records, online engagement, and
confidential prayer requests, to identify members
who may be in need of additional support. For
instance, if a regular attendee misses several Sundays
in a row and has recently submitted a prayer request
about a health issue, the system flags this for pastoral
follow-up.

The AI also assists in matching members with
appropriate care resources. If someone expresses
interest in addiction recovery support, CareAssist can
automatically provide information about relevant

church programs and local Christian counseling services.

Pastor John Martinez reports, "CareAssist has been a tremendous help in ensuring no one falls through the cracks. It's like having an extra set of eyes and ears, helping us to be more proactive in our care. Of course, it doesn't replace the personal touch of our pastoral team, but it does help us allocate our time and resources more effectively."

The church faced challenges in implementing this system, particularly around data privacy and the need to maintain the personal, relational aspect of pastoral care. They addressed these concerns by establishing clear guidelines for data use, ensuring transparency with the congregation, and always having human oversight of the AI's recommendations.

One unexpected benefit of the system was its ability to identify emerging trends in the congregation's needs. For example, CareAssist noticed an increase in prayer requests related to anxiety and work stress among young professionals in the church. This insight led to the development of a new support group and a sermon series addressing work-life balance from a Christian perspective.

This case study illustrates how AI can enhance pastoral care, aligning with the biblical mandate to shepherd the flock (1 Peter 5:2-3). However, it also highlights the importance of maintaining human oversight and addressing ethical concerns, topics we'll explore more deeply in Chapter 13.

Case Study 2: AI in Bible Translation with Wycliffe Bible Translators

Wycliffe Bible Translators, a global organization dedicated to translating the Bible into every language, has been exploring the use of AI to accelerate their work. Their project, called "AI for Bible Translation," uses machine learning algorithms to assist human translators in the complex task of Bible translation.

The AI system, trained on existing translations and linguistic data, can provide initial draft translations and suggest alternatives for difficult passages. This significantly speeds up the translation process, especially for languages with similar structures to those already in the system.

Dr. Sarah Chen, a lead researcher on the project, explains, "AI doesn't replace our translators, but it does make their work more efficient. It's particularly helpful for the initial drafting stage and for checking consistency across the translation. Our human translators then refine these drafts, ensuring accuracy and cultural appropriateness."

One of the most significant benefits has been in translating for languages with limited existing linguistic resources. The AI system can leverage data from related languages to provide initial translations, giving human translators a starting point even for languages they might not be fully fluent in.

However, the project has faced challenges, particularly in dealing with idiomatic expressions and cultural nuances that AI struggles to capture. The team has had to develop careful review processes to ensure that the AI-assisted translations maintain the depth and richness of the original text.

An unexpected benefit of the project has been its ability to identify potential errors or inconsistencies in existing translations. By comparing multiple translations across languages, the AI has sometimes flagged passages where human translators may have introduced unintended variations in meaning.

This case study demonstrates how AI can support the fulfillment of the Great Commission (Matthew 28:19-20) by accelerating Bible translation efforts. It also underscores the continued importance of human expertise in ensuring the accuracy and cultural relevance of translations.

Case Study 3: AI-Powered Community Outreach at Citylight Church in Chicago

Citylight Church in Chicago has implemented an AI-driven community needs assessment tool to enhance their local outreach efforts. The system, which they call "NeedMap," analyzes public data on poverty rates, education levels, health statistics, and other factors to identify areas of greatest need in their community.

NeedMap also incorporates data from the church's own interactions with the community, including food bank usage, attendance at community events, and requests for assistance. This combination of public and church-specific data provides a comprehensive picture of community needs.

Pastor Lisa Wong shares, "NeedMap has transformed our approach to community service. It helps us see beyond our assumptions and really understand where we can have the most impact. For example, we discovered a pocket of elderly residents who were struggling with food insecurity but weren't connected to existing support systems. This insight led us to start a meal delivery program specifically for seniors."

The church has had to navigate challenges related to data interpretation and the risk of reducing complex social issues to mere data points. They've addressed this by combining the AI insights with on-the-ground community engagement, ensuring that their outreach efforts are both data-informed and personally connected.

One unexpected outcome of using NeedMap was the identification of a need for English as a Second Language (ESL) classes in a nearby neighborhood with a growing immigrant population. The church partnered with local schools to offer these classes, which not only met a community need but also opened doors for building relationships and sharing the Gospel.

This case study illustrates how AI can enhance a church's ability to love and serve its neighbors effectively (Mark 12:31), while also highlighting the importance of combining technological insights with personal engagement.

Case Study 4: AI in Worship and Music Ministry at Evangel Cathedral in Maryland

Evangel Cathedral in Maryland has integrated AI into their music ministry through a system they call "WorshipAI." This tool assists in various aspects of worship planning and execution, from song selection to live performance support.

WorshipAI analyzes the church's song database along with factors like the sermon topic, church calendar, and past usage to suggest appropriate worship sets. During live performances, it can provide real-time chord and lyric prompts to worship team members and adjust sound levels based on the acoustics of the room and the size of the congregation.

Music Director James Thompson notes, "WorshipAI has been a game-changer for our team. It helps us create more cohesive, meaningful worship experiences and allows our musicians to focus more on their performance and spiritual connection rather than technical details."

The system has also assisted in songwriting, suggesting chord progressions and even lyrical phrases based on specific themes or biblical passages. This has led to the creation of several original worship songs that resonate deeply with the congregation.

However, the church has had to be mindful of not letting technology overshadow the spiritual essence of worship. They've maintained a balance by using AI as a support tool while emphasizing the importance of Spirit-led worship and personal preparation among their team members.

An unexpected benefit of WorshipAI has been its ability to help integrate new team members more quickly. The system's prompts and suggestions have helped less experienced musicians contribute meaningfully to the worship team, fostering a more inclusive music ministry.

This case study shows how AI can enhance worship experiences, aligning with the biblical call to "sing to the Lord a new song" (Psalm 96:1). It also highlights the need to balance technological assistance with spiritual authenticity in worship.

Case Study 5: AI-Enhanced Discipleship at Life Church

Life Church, a multi-site church known for its
technological innovation, has developed an AI-
powered discipleship app called "GrowthPath." This
app creates personalized spiritual growth plans for
users based on their responses to assessments, their
engagement with biblical content, and their stated
goals.

GrowthPath suggests daily devotionals, Bible reading
plans, and spiritual exercises tailored to each user's
spiritual maturity level and areas of interest or
struggle. It also connects users with relevant small
groups and ministry opportunities within the church.

Pastor Craig Groeschel explains, "GrowthPath is like
having a personal spiritual coach in your pocket. It
helps our members take intentional steps in their faith
journey, providing encouragement and accountability
along the way."

The app uses natural language processing to analyze users' journal entries and prayers, offering encouraging scripture verses or suggesting relevant resources based on the themes and emotions expressed. It also tracks user engagement and progress, adjusting recommendations to maintain an appropriate level of challenge and support.

The church has had to navigate concerns about the depersonalization of discipleship and the risk of reducing spiritual growth to a series of tasks. They've addressed these issues by emphasizing that the app is a supplement to, not a replacement for, personal mentorship and community involvement.

One unexpected outcome has been the app's ability to identify emerging leaders within the church. By analyzing engagement patterns and the content of users' reflections, GrowthPath has helped identify individuals who show potential for various ministry roles, aiding in the church's leadership development efforts.

This case study demonstrates how AI can support personalized discipleship, aligning with Paul's approach of becoming "all things to all people" (1 Corinthians 9:22). It also raises important questions about the role of technology in spiritual formation, a topic we'll explore further in Chapter 13.

Case Study 6: VisitorReach—Digital Outreach Revolution

VisitorReach is a cutting-edge digital outreach platform developed specifically for churches, co-founded by industry leaders including Howard Rachinski (founder of Christian Copyright Licensing International, CCLI), Jeff Carson (Amazon Web Services APN Ambassador and AI strategist), Marc Estes (former Senior Pastor at Mannahouse), and Poncho Lowder (founder of Custom Church Apps). This platform leverages artificial intelligence to help churches move beyond traditional marketing strategies and into personalized, one-on-one SMS conversations with potential visitors, effectively fostering meaningful connections that lead to increased attendance and deeper engagement with the church community.

Unlike conventional church outreach methods, which often rely on mass advertising or digital impressions, VisitorReach uses its proprietary aiChurchTech™ system to target spiritual seekers, those new to an area, or individuals who have left church but may be looking to reconnect. By employing artificial intelligence, the platform identifies these individuals and connects them with local churches through highly personalized SMS conversations. These conversations are central to VisitorReach's philosophy of outreach, as they allow churches to maintain ongoing, meaningful interactions before potential visitors even walk through the doors. The SMS-based communication ensures that these interactions feel personal and engaging, helping to build trust and a relationship over time.

VisitorReach's NurturePoint™ strategy is another key aspect of its effectiveness. Through this strategy, the platform helps churches foster between 100 and 200 new connections monthly, which typically results in 40 to 80 new families visiting the church. These interactions often span months, with many first-time visitors indicating that the continued text-based engagement encouraged them to eventually attend in person. This type of sustained outreach helps churches go beyond mere visitor numbers and focus on developing deeper, more meaningful relationships with those seeking spiritual connection.

Once a visitor does attend, VisitorReach's capabilities don't end. The platform also supports a structured 90-day follow-up process, designed to help integrate new attendees into the church community. This follow-up ensures that visitors feel welcomed, engaged, and involved in the life of the church, increasing the likelihood that they will return and ultimately become regular members. Through this seamless follow-up journey, the platform aids churches in both growing their congregations and maintaining long-term connections with those they engage.

What sets VisitorReach apart is the synergy between AI and human interaction. While the platform automates certain aspects of outreach and engagement—such as sending pre-approved automated messages and managing ongoing conversations—it ensures that the personal touch remains a priority. Church leaders can still directly engage with individuals through one-on-one conversations, crafting personalized responses where necessary. This balance between AI-driven efficiency and human interaction allows pastors to focus on building real relationships without becoming overwhelmed by administrative tasks. In fact, many pastors using the platform have found that it frees up significant time for them to focus on more relational and spiritual aspects of ministry.

With VisitorReach, the founders have created a platform that not only aids in church growth but also ensures the personal and spiritual connections at the heart of ministry remain intact. The team behind VisitorReach—leaders with extensive experience in both ministry and technology—has developed a system that addresses the growing need for churches to adapt to a digital-first world. By combining the efficiency of AI with the authenticity of personal pastoral care, VisitorReach has become an essential tool for churches looking to increase engagement, attendance, and spiritual impact.

Case Study 7: AI-Driven Spiritual Support on Fight Lust (fightlust.com)

FightLust.com is a Christian ministry dedicated to supporting individuals battling lust, pornography, and sexual addiction. People worldwide visit the website at all hours, seeking prayer and guidance. To meet this constant demand, Fight Lust employs an AI-powered chatbot, affectionately known as Jeff, through the platform tawk.to. Jeff engages users by providing immediate spiritual support, leveraging natural language processing (NLP) to detect keywords like "repentance" and "temptation," and delivering relevant prayers and scripture-based advice. This AI-driven system allows people to receive help 24/7, especially when human counselors are not available.

The chatbot is crucial in addressing deep personal struggles. By recognizing specific user inputs, Jeff tailors prayers and guidance to each individual's needs, offering support for repentance, healing, and transformation. It also encourages users to email the ministry for one-on-one prayer, blending AI efficiency with personal engagement.

With users accessing the site from different time zones, Jeff provides real-time spiritual care, fostering an environment of privacy and non-judgmental

119

support. Many people reach out during the night when temptation may be strongest, and this continuous access to the chatbot ensures they receive guidance when they need it most. This global availability makes the chatbot a vital resource in the battle against sexual addiction, helping users resist temptation and pursue recovery.

Jeff plays a pivotal role in users' spiritual journeys by offering tailored support in moments of vulnerability. The chatbot helps users connect with their faith through personalized prayers and guidance rooted in Christian values. As users interact with Jeff, they are guided through steps of repentance and restoration, encouraging them to stay committed to a path of purity and holiness. This technology, combined with the ministry's global reach and constant availability, has a profound impact on helping individuals overcome addiction.

For more detailed examples of chatbot conversations and to see how Jeff interacts with users, please visit fightlust.com/example. Here, real chat transcripts from Fight Lust demonstrate the chatbot's functionality and personalized spiritual support. These transcripts showcase Jeff's ability to adapt its responses based on the specific struggles shared by the users.

As we reflect on these case studies, we see both the potential and the challenges of implementing AI in ministry contexts. While AI offers powerful tools for enhancing various aspects of church life, its use also raises important ethical and theological questions. How do we ensure that our use of AI aligns with our values and mission? How do we maintain the relational and spiritual essence of ministry while leveraging these technological tools?

These are complex questions that require careful consideration. While we've touched on some ethical considerations in these case studies, a more comprehensive discussion of the ethical implications of AI in ministry can be found in Chapter 13. There, we'll explore in depth how to navigate the ethical dilemmas that arise from the use of AI in religious contexts.

As we conclude this chapter on the relevance and benefits of AI in ministry, let's remember the words of the prophet Isaiah: "See, I am doing a new thing! Now it springs up; do you not perceive it? I am making a way in the wilderness and streams in the wasteland" (Isaiah 43:19). AI represents a "new thing" in our ministerial landscape. May we have the wisdom to perceive the opportunities it presents and the discernment to navigate the challenges it poses, always seeking to use these tools for the glory of God and the advancement of His kingdom.

In the next chapter, we'll provide practical guidance on how to use this book effectively, ensuring that you can apply the insights gained from these case studies and discussions to your own ministry context. As we move forward, may we always keep in mind that technology, including AI, is a tool to enhance, not replace, the fundamentally relational and spiritual nature of Christian ministry.

CHAPTER THREE

How to Use This Book

Section 3.1: Navigating the Book's Content

As we embark on this exploration of Artificial
Intelligence (AI) in ministry, it's crucial to understand
how to navigate and make the most of this book's
content. This section serves as your guide, helping
you to effectively engage with the material and apply
it to your ministry context with diligence and
discernment.

First and foremost, if you need a refresher on the
overall structure of the book and its progression from
foundational concepts to practical applications, please
refer back to Chapter 1. There, you'll find a detailed
explanation of how each chapter builds upon the
previous ones, providing a comprehensive
understanding of how AI can be integrated into
various aspects of ministry work.

Now, let's focus on some practical tips for navigating and using this book effectively:

1.   Pray and Reflect

Before diving into each chapter, take a moment to pray for wisdom and discernment. As Proverbs 3:5-6 reminds us, "Trust in the Lord with all your heart and lean not on your own understanding; in all your ways submit to him, and he will make your paths straight." Ask God to guide your understanding and application of the content.

2.   Active Reading

As you read, keep a notebook or digital document handy. Jot down key insights, questions that arise, and potential applications for your specific ministry context. This active engagement will help you internalize the content and make it more relevant to your work.

3.   Scripture Connection

Throughout the book, you'll find Scripture references that provide a biblical foundation for our discussions of AI in ministry. Take time to look up these verses in their full context. Consider how they apply to the technological concepts being discussed.

4. Engage with Examples

Pay special attention to the real-world examples and case studies provided. These are designed to illustrate how AI can be practically applied in ministry settings. As you read these, ask yourself: How might similar approaches work in my context?

5. Utilize Cross-References

When you come across a concept that's briefly mentioned but more fully explored in another chapter, use the cross-references provided to jump to that section for a deeper understanding if needed.

6.   Glossary and AI for Novices

Don't let unfamiliar terms bog you down. Use the glossary at the back of the book for quick reference. For deeper technical explanations, refer to our companion book, "AI for Novices," which is referenced throughout this text.

7.   Reflection Questions

At the end of each chapter, you'll find reflection questions. Take time to thoughtfully consider and answer these. They're designed to help you apply the concepts to your specific ministry context.

8.   Group Discussion

Consider reading this book with a group of fellow ministry leaders. The complex issues surrounding AI in ministry benefit from diverse perspectives and collective wisdom.

9.   Practical Application

After each chapter, identify at least one concrete step you can take to apply what you've learned in your ministry. This could be as simple as researching an AI tool or initiating a conversation with your leadership team about potential AI applications.

10.   Ethical Considerations

As you explore AI applications, always keep ethical considerations in mind. Chapter 13 provides a comprehensive discussion on this topic, but it's important to view all content through an ethical lens.

11.   Pace Yourself

The content of this book is rich and sometimes complex. Don't rush through it. Give yourself time to digest and reflect on each section before moving on.

12.   Revisit and Review

Feel free to jump back to previous chapters as needed. The interconnected nature of AI in ministry means that later chapters often build on earlier concepts.

Remember, the goal of this book is not just to impart information but to equip you to integrate AI into your ministry work thoughtfully. As you read, continually ask yourself: How might this apply in my context? What opportunities does this present? What challenges might I need to address?

In the words of C.S. Lewis, "God is no fonder of intellectual slackers than of any other slackers. If you are thinking of becoming a Christian, I warn you, you are embarking on something which is going to take the whole of you, brains and all." Approaching this book with intellectual rigor and spiritual discernment will help you make the most of its content.

As we move forward, may your engagement with this material be guided by the wisdom of James 1:5: "If any of you lacks wisdom, you should ask God, who gives generously to all without finding fault, and it will be given to you." Let this journey into AI and ministry be one of discovery, growth, and, ultimately, enhanced service to God and His people.

Section 3.2: How Each Section Builds on Christian Principles

As we delve deeper into the intersection of faith and technology, it's crucial to remember that every section of this book is firmly rooted in Christian principles. In Chapter 1.3, we explored the biblical basis for embracing technology in ministry, and Chapter 2 further expanded on why AI is relevant to our calling as followers of Christ. Rather than restating these foundational concepts, let's focus on how to practically apply these principles as you engage with each section of this book.

1. Prayerful Engagement

Before diving into each chapter, take a moment to pray. Ask God for wisdom and discernment as you explore how AI can be used in ministry. James 1:5 reminds us, "If any of you lacks wisdom, you should ask God, who gives generously to all without finding fault, and it will be given to you." This prayerful approach ensures that your engagement with AI is guided by the Holy Spirit.

Practical tip: Create a prayer journal specifically for your journey through this book. Before reading each section, write down your prayers and reflections. After reading, note any insights or applications you've gleaned.

2. Scriptural Reflection

As you read each section, pay close attention to the Scripture references provided. These aren't mere proof texts, but invitations to deeper reflection on how God's Word speaks to our use of technology.

Practical tip: For each chapter, choose one key Scripture reference and spend time meditating on it.

Consider how this verse or passage informs your understanding of AI in ministry. You might use the SOAP method (Scripture, Observation, Application, Prayer) to structure your reflection.

3. Stewardship Mindset

Remember that our engagement with AI, like all aspects of ministry, should be approached from a perspective of stewardship. We are called to be wise stewards of the resources and opportunities God provides, including technological advancements.

Practical tip: As you explore each AI application discussed in the book, ask yourself: "How can this tool help us be better stewards of our time, resources, and ministry opportunities?" Keep a running list of potential stewardship benefits and challenges for each AI application you encounter.

4. Mission-Centric Focus

Every consideration of AI in ministry should be filtered through the lens of our core mission as followers of Christ. As you read each section, continually ask how the discussed technologies align with the Great Commission (Matthew 28:19-20) and the Great Commandment (Matthew 22:36-40).

Practical tip: Create a mission alignment checklist. For each AI application or concept you encounter, evaluate how it supports:

- Evangelism and discipleship
- Loving God and loving others
- Building community
- Serving the needy
- Equipping believers for ministry

5. Ethical Considerations

While we'll dive deep into ethical considerations in Chapter 13, it's important to keep ethical questions at the forefront throughout your reading. Each section should prompt you to consider the ethical implications of AI in ministry.

Practical tip: Start an "Ethical Considerations" document. As you read each chapter, jot down potential ethical concerns or questions that arise. This will prepare you for a more in-depth exploration when you reach Chapter 13.

6. Cultural Relevance

As we explore AI in ministry, we must balance timeless biblical truths with the need for cultural relevance. Paul's approach of becoming "all things to all people" (1 Corinthians 9:22) provides a model for engaging with contemporary tools while maintaining our core message.

Practical tip: For each AI application discussed, consider both its potential for enhancing cultural relevance and any risks of compromising biblical principles. Create a pros and cons list to help you evaluate each tool critically.

7. Community Engagement

Remember that discernment in using AI for ministry isn't a solitary task. The body of Christ is meant to work together, sharing wisdom and insights.

Practical tip: Form a small group or discussion circle with other ministry leaders to work through this book together. Meet regularly to share insights, challenges, and potential applications of AI in your respective ministry contexts.

8. Practical Application

Each section of this book should move you from
theory to practice. Don't just absorb information; look
for ways to apply what you're learning in your specific
ministry context.

Practical tip: After each chapter, write down at least
three concrete steps you can take to explore or
implement the AI applications discussed. These might
range from researching specific tools to initiating
conversations with your leadership team about
potential AI integration.

9. Holistic Ministry Perspective

As you engage with each section, consider how AI can
enhance various aspects of ministry, from pastoral
care to administration, from outreach to worship.
Maintain a holistic view of ministry as you explore
these technologies.

Practical tip: Create a ministry impact matrix. List different areas of your ministry (e.g., pastoral care, evangelism, discipleship, worship, administration) and note how each AI application might impact these areas, both positively and potentially negatively.

10. Personal Spiritual Growth

While the focus of this book is on ministry applications, don't neglect the potential impact of AI on your personal spiritual growth and leadership development.

Practical tip: Keep a personal reflection journal as you read. For each chapter, note not only how the content applies to your ministry but also how it challenges or enhances your personal walk with Christ and your leadership approach.

11. Balancing Efficiency and Relationship

As you explore AI applications in each section, maintain a balance between leveraging technology for efficiency and preserving the relational essence of Christian ministry.

Practical tip: For each AI tool or concept discussed, ask yourself two questions:

1. How can this enhance our efficiency or effectiveness in ministry?

2. How might this impact our personal connections and relationships within the church community?

12. Future-Oriented Thinking

While engaging with current AI applications, also consider the future implications of these technologies for ministry.

Practical tip: After each chapter, spend some time brainstorming potential future developments in AI that could impact ministry. How might the concepts you've just learned evolve in the coming years, and how can your ministry prepare for these changes?

13. Contextual Application

Remember that not every AI application will be suitable for every ministry context. As you read each section, consider how the concepts might be adapted to fit your specific church or organization.

Practical tip: Create a contextual relevance scale from 1-10 for each AI application you encounter. Rate how relevant and applicable each tool or concept is to your specific ministry context, and note any adaptations that might be necessary.

14. Interdisciplinary Connections

As you work through each section, look for connections between AI applications and other disciplines or areas of study that might enhance your ministry.

Practical tip: Keep a list of interdisciplinary connections. For example, how might AI in ministry intersect with psychology, sociology, or educational theory? These connections can provide rich insights for applying AI in nuanced, effective ways.

15. Testimonial Collection

As you begin to implement ideas from the book, start collecting testimonies and case studies from your own ministry context.

Practical tip: Create a shared document or folder where team members can contribute stories of how AI has impacted your ministry. This will help you track the real-world impact of what you're learning and provide encouragement for continued exploration.

16. Continuous Learning Commitment

The field of AI is rapidly evolving. Commit to ongoing learning beyond the contents of this book.

Practical tip: At the end of each chapter, list three additional resources (books, articles, conferences, online courses) that you can explore to deepen your understanding of the topics discussed.

17. Spirit-Led Discernment

Above all, remember that while AI can be a powerful tool, true wisdom and discernment come from the Holy Spirit. As John reminds us in 1 John 4:1, "Dear friends, do not believe every spirit, but test the spirits to see whether they are from God."

Practical tip: For each AI application you consider implementing, set aside time for prayer and seeking the Spirit's guidance. Create a discernment checklist that includes questions like:

- Does this align with Scripture?
- Does it serve our mission?
- Have we sought wise counsel?
- Do we have peace about this decision?

Applying these practical strategies as you engage with each section of the book'll ensure that your exploration of AI in ministry remains grounded in Christian principles. Remember, the goal is not just to understand AI, but to use it wisely and effectively in service of God's kingdom.

As we move forward, may your engagement with this material be guided by Paul's exhortation in Philippians 1:9-10: "And this is my prayer: that your love may abound more and more in knowledge and depth of insight, so that you may be able to discern what is best and may be pure and blameless for the day of Christ."

In the next section, we'll provide practical guidance for implementing AI in ministry, building on the principles and strategies we've discussed here. As we do so, may we always remember that our ultimate goal is not technological sophistication, but faithful and effective service to God and His people.

Section 3.3: Practical Guidance for Implementing AI in Ministry

As we conclude this chapter on how to use this book, it's essential to provide practical guidance for implementing AI in ministry. While we've explored the benefits and potential applications of AI in Chapter 2, here we'll focus on the concrete steps you can take to begin integrating AI into your ministry context. Remember, this is a journey of faithful innovation, and as Proverbs 16:9 reminds us, "In their hearts humans plan their course, but the Lord establishes their steps."

1. Assessment and Prayer

The first step in implementing AI in your ministry should always be prayerful assessment. Before rushing to adopt any new technology, take time to seek God's guidance and carefully evaluate your ministry's needs and readiness for AI integration.

Key questions to consider:

- What are the current challenges in our ministry that AI might help address?
- How might AI enhance our ability to fulfill our mission and serve our community?
- What resources (financial, technical, human) do we have available for AI implementation?
- What potential risks or concerns should we be aware of?

Refer to Section 2.1 in Chapter 2 for a deeper exploration of how AI can address specific ministry needs.

2. Education and Understanding

Once you've identified potential areas for AI implementation, ensure that you and your team have a solid understanding of the technology you're considering. This book serves as a starting point, but you may need to seek additional resources or expertise depending on your specific plans.

Action steps:

- Encourage key staff and volunteers to engage with relevant sections of this book.
- Consider organizing study groups or workshops to discuss the implications of AI for your ministry.
- If needed, seek additional training or consultation from experts in the field.

Remember, this educational process must include not just the technical aspects of AI, but also the ethical and theological considerations we've discussed throughout this book.

3. Start Small and Pilot

When it comes to implementing AI in ministry, it's often wise to start small and scale up gradually.

Choose a specific area or project for your initial AI implementation.

Suggestions for starting points:

- Using an AI tool for sermon research or preparation
- Implementing a chatbot on your church website for basic inquiries
- Using AI analytics to understand patterns in church attendance or engagement

Treat this as a pilot project, allowing you to learn and adjust before wider implementation. Set clear goals for your pilot project, and establish metrics to measure its effectiveness. These could include quantitative measures (like increased engagement or efficiency) and qualitative feedback from staff and congregation members.

Refer to the case studies in Section 2.3 of Chapter 2 for examples of how other churches have successfully piloted AI projects.

4. Ensure Ethical Use

As you implement AI in your ministry, it's crucial to establish clear ethical guidelines. These should be grounded in biblical principles and reflect your church's values.

Key ethical considerations:

- Data privacy and security
- Transparency about AI use
- Safeguards against potential misuse or over-reliance on AI
- Ensuring AI use doesn't diminish the human and relational aspects of ministry

Develop a code of ethics for AI use in your ministry, drawing on the ethical considerations discussed throughout this book. For a more comprehensive discussion on navigating ethical dilemmas in AI implementation, refer to Chapter 13.

5. Train Your Team

Effective implementation of AI in ministry requires not just leaders who understand the technology but also a team equipped to use it effectively. Invest in training for your staff and key volunteers.

Training approaches:

- Formal courses or workshops
- Hands-on learning experiences
- Regular updates and discussions about AI developments and their implications for ministry

Encourage a culture of continuous learning and adaptation. As AI technology evolves rapidly, your team will need to stay informed about new developments and potential applications.

6. Communicate with Your Congregation

Transparency and clear communication are essential when implementing new technologies in ministry. Take time to explain to your congregation why you're using AI, how it will be used, and what safeguards are in place.

Communication strategies:

- Sermons or teaching series on faith and technology
- Articles in church newsletters or bulletins
- Open forums or Q&A sessions about AI implementation

Address any concerns or misconceptions proactively. Some members may be hesitant about technology in ministry, while others might have unrealistic expectations about what AI can do. Provide opportunities for questions and feedback.

7. Monitor, Evaluate, and Adjust

Once you've implemented AI in a specific area of your ministry, monitoring its impact closely is crucial. Regularly evaluate whether the AI solution meets your goals and aligns with your values. Be prepared to make adjustments as needed.

Evaluation methods:

- Regular surveys of staff, volunteers, and congregation members
- Analysis of quantitative data (e.g., engagement metrics, efficiency improvements)

- Qualitative feedback through interviews or focus groups

Seek feedback from various stakeholders. Pay attention not just to efficiency metrics but also to how AI use is affecting the spiritual and relational aspects of your ministry.

8. Scale Thoughtfully

If your initial AI implementation proves successful, consider expanding its use to other areas of ministry. Do so thoughtfully and gradually. Each new application of AI should undergo the same assessment, planning, and careful implementation.

Scaling considerations:

- Prioritize areas where AI can have the most significant positive impact
- Consider the cumulative effect of multiple AI implementations on your overall ministry
- Continuously reassess the balance between technological efficiency and relational ministry

As you scale, be mindful of the potential for AI to reshape aspects of your ministry in unintended ways. Always keep your core mission and values at the forefront, using AI as a tool to enhance, not redefine, your ministry.

9. Stay Informed and Adaptable

The field of AI is rapidly evolving, with new capabilities and applications emerging regularly. Stay informed about these developments and be willing to adapt your approach as new opportunities or challenges arise.

Strategies for staying informed:

- Designate someone on your team to keep abreast of AI developments relevant to ministry
- Attend conferences or webinars on AI and faith
- Engage with other churches or ministries using AI to share insights and best practices

Regularly revisit and update your AI strategy. This aligns with the biblical principle of wisdom and discernment, as expressed in Proverbs 1:5, "let the wise listen and add to their learning, and let the discerning get guidance."

10. Maintain a Christ-Centered Focus

Throughout the process of implementing AI in your ministry, it's crucial to maintain a Christ-centered focus. Remember that AI is a tool to help us fulfill our mission more effectively, not an end in itself.

Guiding questions:

- How does this AI implementation help us love God and love others more effectively?
- Are we using AI in a way that honors God and serves His people?
- Does our use of AI align with the teachings of Jesus and the mission of the church?

Regularly revisit your reasons for using AI and ensure they align with your calling to share the gospel and make disciples.

Practical Considerations for Specific Ministry Areas

While the above principles apply broadly to AI implementation in ministry, let's consider some specific guidance for different areas of ministry:

Pastoral Care

If AI is implemented in pastoral care (such as through chatbots or data analysis), ensure that it complements rather than replaces personal, human care. Use AI to identify needs and provide initial support, but always have clear pathways for human follow-up.

Worship and Music

When using AI in worship planning or music creation, be mindful of the need for authentic, Spirit-led worship. Use AI as a tool to enhance creativity and efficiency, but not at the expense of genuine expression and participation.

Preaching and Teaching

AI can be a powerful tool for sermon preparation and Bible study, but it should never replace the preacher's personal engagement with Scripture and reliance on the Holy Spirit. Use AI to enhance your study and preparation but ensure that your messages remain personally crafted and Spirit-led.

Administration

In church administration, AI can significantly improve efficiency and data management. However, be careful not to let data-driven decision-making override pastoral wisdom and the directives of the Holy Spirit. Use AI to inform, not dictate, your administrative choices.

Outreach and Evangelism

AI can help target and personalize outreach efforts, but remember that genuine evangelism is relational and Spirit-led. Use AI to identify opportunities and optimize communication, but ensure that your outreach maintains a personal touch and authentic witness.

As you implement AI in these and other areas of ministry, always keep in mind the words of Paul in 1 Corinthians 9:22-23, "I have become all things to all people so that by all possible means I might save some. I do all this for the sake of the gospel, that I may share in its blessings." AI is a new means by which we can reach people and enhance our ministry, but the ultimate purpose remains unchanged -- to share the gospel and bring people into a relationship with Christ.

Implementing AI in ministry is not about chasing the latest trends or trying to appear cutting-edge. It's about thoughtfully and prayerfully leveraging new tools to fulfill our God-given mission more effectively. As you move forward in this process, may you be guided by the wisdom of Proverbs 16:3, "Commit to the Lord whatever you do, and he will establish your plans."

Remember that the goal of all our ministry efforts, including our use of AI, is to glorify God and make disciples. As you implement AI in your ministry, continually ask yourself: How does this help us love God more deeply? How does it enable us to love our neighbors more effectively? How does it contribute to the Great Commission of making disciples?

Be patient with yourself and your team as you navigate this new territory. Implementation will likely involve some trial and error, and that's okay. Learn from your successes and setbacks, always keeping your eyes fixed on Jesus, "the pioneer and perfecter of faith" (Hebrews 12:2).

Stay connected with other ministry leaders who are on similar journeys. Share your experiences, learn from others, and contribute to the broader conversation about faith and technology in the church.

Above all, remain committed to prayer throughout this process. Seek God's wisdom, guidance, and blessing on your efforts. Trust that He who called you to ministry will equip you for the task, even as the tools and methods evolve.

May your journey of implementing AI in ministry be marked by wisdom, discernment, and, above all, a deep reliance on the guidance of the Holy Spirit. As you navigate this new frontier, may you experience the truth of James 1:5, "If any of you lacks wisdom, you should ask God, who gives generously to all without finding fault, and it will be given to you."

PART ONE

PART I: UNDERSTANDING AI IN A MINISTRY CONTEXT

CHAPTER FOUR

What is Artificial Intelligence?

Section 4.1: A Layman's Introduction to AI

Imagine, for a moment, that you're sitting in your church office, preparing for next Sunday's sermon. You've got your well-worn Bible open, a stack of commentaries at your side, and a blank document on your computer screen. Now, picture having an intelligent assistant right there with you – one that could instantly recall every verse in the Bible, cross-reference theological concepts, and even suggest relevant illustrations for your message. This assistant never tires, never forgets, and is available 24/7. Sounds like science fiction, doesn't it? Welcome to the world of Artificial Intelligence (AI) in ministry.

But what exactly is AI? Let's start our journey into understanding this transformative technology by breaking it down in simple, everyday terms.

At its core, Artificial Intelligence is like creating a digital brain – a computer system designed to perform tasks that typically require human intelligence. These tasks might include understanding and responding to human language, recognizing patterns, learning from experience, and making decisions. It's as if we've given computers the ability to think, reason, and in some ways, understand the world around them.

Now, you might be wondering, "Is this something new? Haven't computers always been 'intelligent'?" The answer lies in the distinction between traditional computing and AI. Traditional computers are incredibly fast calculators – they can process vast amounts of data and perform complex mathematical operations in the blink of an eye. But they can only do exactly what they're programmed to do. If a situation arises that wasn't accounted for in their programming, they're stumped.

AI, on the other hand, is designed to adapt and learn. It's like the difference between memorizing a list of Bible verses and truly understanding the deeper meaning and context of Scripture. AI systems can take in new information, learn from it, and apply that knowledge to new situations – much like how we, as humans, learn and grow in our faith and understanding.

Let's use a biblical analogy to further illustrate this concept. In the book of Daniel, we read about Daniel interpreting Nebuchadnezzar's dream. Daniel not only had to provide the interpretation but also describe the dream itself, which the king had forgotten. This required not just recalling information but understanding, insight, and the ability to piece together complex elements – abilities that go beyond simple data retrieval.

In a similar way, AI systems are designed to go beyond mere information retrieval. They can analyze complex situations, draw insights, and even make predictions based on the data they've been trained on. It's as if we've created digital assistants that can, in their own way, interpret the 'dreams' of our modern world.

But let's be clear – AI is not magic, and it's certainly not omniscient like our Creator. It's a tool, albeit powerful, created by human ingenuity and built upon decades of technological advancements. Just as we use other tools in our ministry – from the printing press that allows us to distribute Bibles to the microphones that amplify our voices during worship – AI is another tool that, when used wisely, can enhance and support our work in spreading the Gospel.

So, how does AI actually work? Without delving too deeply into the technical details (remember, we have our companion book "AI for Novices" for those), let's consider a simple analogy.

Imagine you're teaching a child to recognize different animals. You might show them pictures of various animals, tell them the names, and describe some key features. Over time, the child learns to identify animals they've never seen before by recognizing patterns and characteristics they've learned. This is essentially how many AI systems learn – through a process called machine learning.

In machine learning, we feed vast amounts of data into the AI system. This data acts like the pictures and descriptions in our animal recognition analogy. The AI then processes this data, identifying patterns and relationships. Over time, it builds a model of understanding that it can apply to new, unseen data.

For instance, if we wanted to create an AI system to help with biblical exegesis, we might feed it thousands of Bible verses, commentaries, and theological texts. The AI would then learn to recognize patterns in language, themes in scripture, and connections between different parts of the Bible. It could draw upon this learned knowledge to offer insights or interpretations when presented with a new verse or passage.

Now, you might be thinking, "This sounds impressive, but can a machine really understand the depths of God's word?" And you'd be right to ask that question. AI, as advanced as it is, doesn't truly 'understand' in the way we do. It doesn't have the spiritual discernment or the personal relationship with God that informs our interpretation of Scripture. What it does have is the ability to process and analyze vast amounts of information at incredible speeds, offering us tools and insights that can support and enhance our own God-given abilities of discernment and interpretation.

Think of AI as a powerful research assistant. It can quickly sift through centuries of biblical scholarship, find relevant cross-references, and even suggest connections we might have missed. But the final interpretation, the application of God's word to our lives and our congregations – that remains the domain of human pastors and leaders, guided by the Holy Spirit.

As we continue to explore AI in this book, it's important to keep this perspective in mind. AI is a tool – a remarkably powerful one, but a tool nonetheless. Like any tool, its value lies not in itself but in how we choose to use it in service of our calling.

In the next section, we'll delve into some common AI technologies that are particularly relevant to ministry. But before we do, let's pause for a moment of reflection.

Consider how technology has already impacted your ministry. Perhaps you use Bible software for study or social media to connect with your congregation. How has this technology enhanced your work? How has it challenged you? As we step into the world of AI, these reflections can help us approach this new technology with wisdom and discernment, always keeping our focus on glorifying God and serving His people.

Section 4.2: Common AI Technologies

As we continue our journey into the world of Artificial Intelligence, let's explore some of the common AI technologies that are particularly relevant to ministry. Just as we use different tools for different tasks in our church work - a microphone for preaching, a keyboard for worship, or a projector for visual aids - AI offers a variety of tools, each suited to different aspects of our ministry.

Before we dive in, let's remind ourselves of the purpose of these tools. In 1 Corinthians 12:7, Paul writes, "Now to each one the manifestation of the Spirit is given for the common good." While Paul was speaking of spiritual gifts, we can apply this principle to the tools and technologies we use in ministry. Our goal in understanding and potentially using AI should always be to serve our congregations better and to spread the Gospel more effectively.

1. Natural Language Processing (NLP)

The first AI technology we'll explore is Natural Language Processing, or NLP. This is perhaps the most immediately applicable AI technology for ministry, as it deals directly with human language - the primary medium through which we communicate God's word.

NLP is like having a linguist, a translator, and a communication expert all rolled into one. It allows computers to understand, interpret, and even generate human language. Think of it as teaching a computer to read and write, not just in one language, but potentially in any language.

In ministry, NLP can be a powerful tool for biblical research and sermon preparation. Imagine being able to search not just for specific words in the Bible, but for concepts or themes. For example, you could ask an NLP system to find all passages related to "God's love" or "forgiveness," and it would understand the context and nuances of these concepts, returning relevant verses even if they don't explicitly use those words.

NLP can also assist in translation work. While it can't replace human translators, especially for the nuanced work of Bible translation, it can provide initial drafts or help check consistency across translations. This could be particularly useful for missionaries working in areas with less common languages.

Another application of NLP in ministry is in creating chatbots for church websites. These AI-powered assistants can answer common questions about service times, church beliefs, or even provide basic spiritual guidance. However, it's crucial to remember that while these can be helpful tools, they should never replace personal pastoral care.

2. Machine Learning and Deep Learning

Next, let's talk about Machine Learning and its more complex cousin, Deep Learning. If NLP is about understanding language, Machine Learning is about understanding patterns and making predictions based on those patterns.

Machine Learning is like having a tireless research assistant who can analyze vast amounts of data and draw insights from it. It works by feeding large amounts of data into an AI system and allowing it to find patterns and relationships within that data.

In a ministry context, Machine Learning could be used to analyze church attendance patterns, giving trends, or engagement with different programs. This could help church leaders make more informed decisions about resource allocation or identify areas where additional pastoral care might be needed.

Deep Learning takes this a step further, using complex neural networks that mimic the human brain to process information. This technology is particularly good at tasks like image and speech recognition.

In a church setting, Deep Learning could be used for things like automatically transcribing sermons, making them searchable and accessible to those who might have missed the service. It could also be used in security systems, helping to ensure the safety of our congregations during gatherings.

However, as we consider these technologies, we must remember the words of Proverbs 3:5-6: "Trust in the Lord with all your heart and lean not on your own understanding; in all your ways submit to him, and he will make your paths straight." While data and analysis can be helpful tools, they should never replace our reliance on God's guidance in leading our churches.

3. Computer Vision

Computer Vision is another AI technology with interesting applications in ministry. This technology allows computers to 'see' and understand visual information from the world around them, much like human vision.

In a church context, Computer Vision could be used to automatically count attendance at services or events, saving time for staff and volunteers. It could also be used in security systems to identify potential safety issues.

More creatively, Computer Vision could be used to enhance accessibility in our churches. For example, it could power systems that automatically generate descriptions of visual elements in sermons or worship services for visually impaired members of the congregation.

However, as with all technologies, we must be mindful of privacy concerns and ensure that our use of such systems aligns with our values of respecting and protecting our congregation members.

4. Generative AI

Generative AI is a fascinating and rapidly evolving area of AI technology. This is the type of AI that can create new content - whether that's text, images, music, or even video.

In ministry, Generative AI could be used to create visual aids for sermons, generate ideas for youth group activities, or even assist in writing church newsletters. Some systems can even generate music, which could potentially be used in worship services (although this raises interesting questions about the role of human creativity in worship, which we'll explore later in this book).

One particularly relevant application of Generative AI for pastors is in sermon preparation. While it should never replace the prayerful consideration and Spirit-led insights that go into crafting a sermon, it could be a useful tool for generating ideas or finding new angles on familiar passages.

For example, you might input a Bible passage and ask the AI to generate a list of potential sermon topics or illustrations related to that passage. Or you could use it to brainstorm creative ways to engage your congregation with a particular biblical truth.

However, we must approach Generative AI with caution and discernment. In 2 Timothy 4:2, Paul exhorts Timothy to "Preach the word; be prepared in season and out of season; correct, rebuke and encourage—with great patience and careful instruction." While AI can be a helpful tool in preparation, the act of preaching - of sharing God's word with His people - remains a deeply human and Spirit-led endeavor.

5. Predictive Analytics

Finally, let's consider Predictive Analytics. This technology uses data, statistical algorithms, and machine learning techniques to identify the likelihood of future outcomes based on historical data.

In a ministry context, Predictive Analytics could be used to anticipate needs within the congregation or community. For example, it might help identify trends in attendance or giving, allowing church leaders to proactively address potential issues. It could also be used in outreach efforts, helping to identify the most effective ways to engage with different groups in the community.

However, as we consider the use of such technology, we must remember the words of James 4:13-15: "Now listen, you who say, 'Today or tomorrow we will go to this or that city, spend a year there, carry on business and make money.' Why, you do not even know what will happen tomorrow. What is your life? You are a mist that appears for a little while and then vanishes.

Instead, you ought to say, 'If it is the Lord's will, we will live and do this or that.'"

While predictive tools can be helpful, we must always remain open to the directives of the Holy Spirit, recognizing that God's plans may not always align with our predictions or expectations.

As we conclude this overview of common AI technologies, it's important to remember that these are just tools. They can enhance our ministry efforts, but they cannot replace the core of what we do - sharing God's love, teaching His word, and caring for His people.

In the next section, we'll explore some of AI's myths and realities, helping us approach this technology with enthusiasm and wisdom. But before we move on, take a moment to reflect on the technologies we've discussed. Can you think of ways these might be applied in your specific ministry context? Are there areas where you see potential benefits? Are there aspects that give you pause?

Remember, our goal is not to become experts in AI, but to understand it well enough to make informed decisions about its use in our ministries. As we continue to explore this topic, let's keep our hearts and minds open to how God might use these new tools to further His kingdom.

Section 4.3: Myths and Realities of AI

As we delve deeper into the world of Artificial Intelligence, it's crucial that we separate fact from fiction. Like any new and powerful technology, AI has been the subject of much speculation, excitement, and even fear. In this section, we'll explore some common myths about AI and contrast them with the realities, always keeping in mind our perspective as ministers of the Gospel.

Let's begin with a reflection from Scripture. In Proverbs 18:15, we read, "The heart of the discerning acquires knowledge, for the ears of the wise seek it out." As we examine these myths and realities, let's approach them with discernment, seeking to understand this technology not for its own sake, but for how it might serve our calling to minister to God's people.

Myth 1: AI Will Replace Human Pastors and Ministers

Perhaps the most concerning myth for those in ministry is the idea that AI could someday replace human pastors and ministers. This fear isn't unique to the church - many professions are grappling with similar concerns about automation.

Reality: AI is a Tool, Not a Replacement

While AI can perform many tasks efficiently, it lacks the essential qualities that make human ministry irreplaceable. AI lacks faith, doesn't experience God's love, and can't form genuine relationships. It can process information, but it can't pray. It can analyze text, but it can't discern the movement of the Holy Spirit.

Consider the words of Paul in 1 Corinthians 2:13-14: "This is what we speak, not in words taught us by human wisdom but in words taught by the Spirit, explaining spiritual realities with Spirit-taught words. The person without the Spirit does not accept the things that come from the Spirit of God but considers them foolishness, and cannot understand them because they are discerned only through the Spirit."

AI, no matter how advanced, cannot replicate the Spirit-led discernment that is crucial to pastoral ministry. Instead of replacing pastors, AI should be seen as a tool to enhance and support their work. For example, AI could help with administrative tasks, freeing up more time for pastors to focus on personal ministry and spiritual guidance.

Myth 2: AI is Infallible and Unbiased

Another common myth is that AI, being based on logic and data, is inherently unbiased and always correct.

Reality: AI Can Inherit and Amplify Human Biases

The truth is that AI systems are created by humans and trained on data generated by humans. As a result, they can inherit and even amplify human biases present in their training data. This is particularly important to consider in ministry contexts, where we deal with diverse communities and sensitive issues.

For instance, an AI system trained primarily on Western theological texts might struggle to understand or represent non-Western Christian perspectives.

When using AI in ministry, we must be aware of these potential biases and work to counteract them. This might involve carefully curating the data used to train AI systems or always having human oversight to check AI outputs for bias or inaccuracy.

Myth 3: AI Understands Meaning and Context Like Humans Do

There's often an assumption that because AI can process language and respond in seemingly intelligent ways, it truly understands the meaning and context of information like humans do.

Reality: AI Processes Patterns, Not Meaning

In reality, even the most advanced AI systems today don't truly understand meaning or context in the way humans do. They are incredibly sophisticated pattern recognition machines, but they don't have the ability to truly comprehend or reason about the information they process.

This is particularly important to remember when dealing with Scripture. An AI can find patterns and connections in biblical text, but it can't understand the deeper spiritual truths or apply them to life situations in the way a human pastor can.

181

As it says in 1 Corinthians 2:11, "For who knows a person's thoughts except their own spirit within them? In the same way no one knows the thoughts of God except the Spirit of God."

When using AI for biblical study or sermon preparation, it should be seen as a research assistant, not an interpreter. The crucial tasks of interpreting Scripture, discerning its application, and communicating God's truth to the congregation remain firmly in the realm of Spirit-led human ministry.

Myth 4: AI Will Solve All Our Problems

There's sometimes a tendency to view AI as a panacea, capable of solving all our problems and challenges in ministry.

Reality: AI is a Powerful Tool, But Not a Cure-All

While AI can certainly help address many challenges in ministry, it's not a magical solution to all problems. It's a tool, and like any tool, its effectiveness depends on how it's used.

For example, AI could help a church better understand giving patterns and potentially increase donations, but it can't instill a spirit of generosity in the congregation. It could help analyze attendance trends, but it can't build a genuine community that makes people want to attend church.

Zechariah 4:6 reminds us, "'Not by might nor by power, but by my Spirit,' says the Lord Almighty." While we can and should use tools like AI to support our ministry, we must always remember that true transformation comes through the work of the Holy Spirit, not through human efforts or technological solutions.

Myth 5: AI is Too Complicated for Non-Experts to Use

There's often a perception that AI is so complex and technical that it's beyond the reach of those who have extensive technical knowledge.

Reality: Many AI Tools Are Becoming User-Friendly

While it's true that developing AI systems requires specialized knowledge, many AI tools are becoming increasingly user-friendly. Just as you don't need to understand the intricacies of internal combustion to drive a car, you don't need to be an AI expert to use AI-powered tools in your ministry.

For example, AI writing assistants can now help draft newsletters or social media posts, AI-powered Bible study tools that can help with research, and AI scheduling systems that can help manage church calendars - all with interfaces designed for non-technical users.

This democratization of AI technology opens up opportunities for churches of all sizes to benefit from these tools. However, it also underscores the importance of digital literacy in modern ministry. As leaders, we should strive to understand these tools well enough to use them effectively and ethically.

As we read in Proverbs 15:14, "The discerning heart seeks knowledge, but the mouth of a fool feeds on folly." Let's approach these new technologies with a discerning heart, seeking to understand them so we can use them wisely in service of our calling.

Myth 6: AI is Something We Can Ignore in Ministry

On the flip side of viewing AI as all-powerful is the myth that AI is irrelevant to ministry and can be safely ignored.

Reality: AI is Increasingly Pervasive and Influential

The reality is that AI is becoming increasingly pervasive in all aspects of society, including the lives of our congregation members. From the smartphones in their pockets to the social media platforms they use, AI is shaping how people access information, communicate, and even think.

As ministers, we need to be aware of these influences. We don't need to become AI experts, but we should understand enough to help our congregations navigate these technologies' ethical and spiritual challenges.

Moreover, as we've discussed throughout this chapter, AI offers many potential benefits for enhancing and supporting our ministry work. Ignoring it entirely means missing out on tools that could help us serve our communities more effectively.

Remember the words of Paul in 1 Corinthians 9:22-23: "I have become all things to all people so that by all possible means I might save some. I do all this for the sake of the gospel, that I may share in its blessings." While Paul wasn't talking about technology, his willingness to adapt his approach to reach people with the Gospel is a principle we can apply to our engagement with new technologies like AI.

As we conclude this exploration of AI myths and realities, let's take a moment to reflect. How have these insights changed your perception of AI? Are there ways you can see AI supporting your ministry while avoiding the pitfalls we've discussed?

Remember, our goal in understanding AI is not to become technologists but to be wise stewards of the tools available to us in spreading the Gospel and caring for God's people. As we move forward, let's continue to approach AI with discernment, always keeping our focus on our true calling - to love God and serve His people.

In the next chapter, we'll explore Biblical perspectives on technology, helping us ground our approach to AI in the timeless wisdom of Scripture. But before we do, take some time to consider how the realities of AI we've discussed might apply in your specific ministry context. Are there areas where AI could help you serve your congregation better? Are there potential pitfalls you need to be aware of?

As always, let's approach these questions prayerfully, seeking God's wisdom as we navigate this new technological frontier.

CHAPTER FIVE

Biblical Perspectives on Technology

Section 5.1: Technology in the Bible

The sacred pages of Scripture unfold a rich tapestry of human innovation interwoven with divine purpose. While the term "artificial intelligence" may be absent from its verses, the Bible resonates with the echoes of technological advancement throughout history.

From the earliest chapters of Genesis, the narrative of human creativity emerges. The world of Tubal-Cain in Genesis 4:22 comes alive with the rhythmic clang of a hammer on an anvil. This first metalworker, forging tools of bronze and iron, represents humanity's initial steps into technological innovation. His creations, though simple by today's standards, were revolutionary in their time - a testament to the image of the Creator reflected in human ingenuity.

C.S. Lewis, in his timeless work "Mere Christianity," draws a compelling parallel between God's creative act and human invention: "God made us: invented us as a man invents an engine. A car is made to run on petrol, and it would not run properly on anything else. Now God designed the human machine to run on Himself." This profound insight reminds us that while human creativity may produce wonders of technology, our ultimate purpose lies in connection with our Creator.

The narrative of technological advancement flows seamlessly through the construction of the Tabernacle and later, Solomon's Temple. Exodus 31 introduces Bezalel, a man "filled with the Spirit of God, with wisdom, with understanding, with knowledge and with all kinds of skills." This passage reveals a God who not only approves of technology but actively endows individuals with the ability to create it. The Tabernacle and Temple stood as marvels of ancient engineering and craftsmanship, their every detail a testament to human skill directed towards divine worship.

John Stott, in his insightful work "Issues Facing Christians Today," reminds readers that "God is not against technology or science; He is the author of the scientific laws that have allowed technological progress." This sentiment reverberates through the intricate details of Solomon's Temple, where enormous bronze pillars and seas showcased not just functionality, but artistry born of advanced metallurgical knowledge and engineering prowess.

The biblical narrative takes an unexpected turn when considering how God often uses seemingly primitive technology to accomplish His purposes. Noah's ark, a feat of ancient shipbuilding, carried the hope of humanity through the deluge. The walls of Jericho crumbled to the sound of trumpets and shouts. A simple sling in the hands of a shepherd boy felled a giant. These accounts serve as powerful reminders that the effectiveness of technology lies not in its sophistication, but in its alignment with God's will.

G.K. Chesterton, with his characteristic wit, once observed in "What's Wrong with the World" that "It isn't that they can't see the solution. It is that they can't see the problem." In our modern context, this insight rings true. The challenge often lies not in a lack of technological capability, but in discerning how best to harness it for Kingdom purposes.

The New Testament era ushered in a new chapter in the story of technology and faith. The vast network of Roman roads, marvels of ancient civil engineering, became highways for the spread of the Gospel. The development of papyrus and parchment enabled the writing and distribution of the Epistles, forming the backbone of early Christian teaching.

The Apostle Paul emerges as a master communicator, leveraging the technology of his day to pastor and teach across vast distances. His letters, which form a significant portion of the New Testament, functioned much like today's emails or blog posts, allowing him to nurture multiple churches simultaneously.

Bill Scheidler, in "The Local Church Today," astutely notes that "God has always used the advancements of man to further His eternal purpose." This divine pattern continues to unfold in our digital age, where artificial intelligence and other technologies offer new avenues for ministry and outreach.

The prophet Isaiah paints a vivid picture that resonates with our modern technological landscape. "They will beat their swords into plowshares and their spears into pruning hooks" (Isaiah 2:4). This powerful imagery of transformation speaks to the potential of repurposing tools for growth and flourishing. In the same spirit, artificial intelligence, social media, and data analytics can be envisioned as modern-day "plowshares," cultivating fertile ground for spiritual growth and community building.

Navigating the complex terrain of modern technology, Paul's words in Titus 1:15 offer guidance: "To the pure, all things are pure, but to those who are corrupted and do not believe, nothing is pure." This principle underscores the neutrality of technology itself. The key lies in the heart and motivation of those wielding it. Even the most advanced artificial intelligence, when guided by pure intentions, can become a powerful tool for spreading God's love and truth.

A.W. Tozer, in his spiritual classic "The Pursuit of God," reminds readers of their ultimate purpose: "God is trying to call us back to that for which He created us, to worship Him and to enjoy Him forever." This truth must remain the North Star as artificial intelligence and other technologies are integrated into ministries. These tools, however advanced, are meant to facilitate, not replace, the fundamental connection with the Divine.

The biblical narrative of technology invites deep reflection on the approach to artificial intelligence in ministry. How can modern church leaders, like Bezalel, ensure that their use of technology is infused with the Spirit of God? In what ways can they follow Paul's example, using the communication tools of the day to spread the Gospel far and wide? How might the "swords" of the digital age be transformed into "plowshares" that nurture spiritual growth?

Standing on the cusp of a new technological frontier, church leaders are not merely adopting new tools. They're continuing a sacred tradition of using human innovation to glorify God and serve His people. The next chapter will delve into the ethics of artificial intelligence from a Christian perspective, building on these biblical foundations.

But before moving forward, consider this: How might God be calling you to use the technological marvels of our age for His eternal purposes? The story of technology in the Bible is not just a historical account, but a living narrative that continues to unfold in the digital age. As pastors and church leaders, you have the opportunity to write the next chapter in this ongoing story of faith and innovation.

The journey through Scripture reveals a God who delights in human creativity and innovation when directed towards His purposes. From the craftsmanship of the Tabernacle to the engineering marvels of Solomon's Temple, from the strategic use of Roman roads to the proliferation of the written word, technology has always played a role in advancing God's kingdom.

Artificial intelligence is now the latest frontier in this long line of technological advancements. Like the tools of biblical times, it holds the potential to be a powerful instrument for ministry when wielded with wisdom and discernment. The challenge and opportunity for today's church leaders lie in harnessing this potential while remaining grounded in timeless biblical principles.

As you prepare to explore the ethical implications of artificial intelligence in ministry, keep in mind the examples set by those who have gone before. Like Bezalel, seek the wisdom and skill that comes from God. Like Paul, be willing to embrace new methods of communication to reach people where they are. And like the prophets of old, maintain a vision of how today's "swords" can be transformed into tomorrow's "plowshares."

The next chapter will guide you through the complex landscape of artificial intelligence ethics, providing a biblical framework for navigating these new waters. It will address questions such as: How do we ensure that our use of artificial intelligence aligns with Christian values? What are the potential pitfalls to avoid? How can we leverage this technology to enhance, rather than replace, human connection and spiritual growth?

As you turn the page to this next crucial topic, remember that you're not alone in this journey. Just as God equipped His people throughout history with the tools they needed for their time, He continues to provide wisdom and guidance for the challenges of today. The story of technology in the Bible is your story too - a story of human creativity meeting divine purpose, of innovation in service of eternal truths.

Section 5.2: The Ethics of AI from a Christian Perspective

Christian leaders find themselves at a unique crossroads in the rapidly evolving landscape of artificial intelligence. The potential benefits of this technology in ministry are vast, yet so too are the ethical considerations that must be carefully navigated. As stewards of both spiritual guidance and technological progress, pastors and church leaders must approach artificial intelligence with a biblically-informed ethical framework.

The foundation of this ethical approach lies in the understanding that all technology, including artificial intelligence, is a tool. Like any tool, its moral value depends on how it is used. As C.S. Lewis astutely observed, "What we call Man's power over Nature turns out to be a power exercised by some men over other men with Nature as its instrument." This insight reminds us that the ethical use of artificial intelligence in ministry is not about the technology itself but about how we choose to wield it.

One of the primary ethical concerns surrounding artificial intelligence is the potential for dehumanization. In a world increasingly mediated by algorithms and automated systems, there's a risk of reducing human beings to mere data points. This stands in stark contrast to the Christian view of humanity as beings created in the image of God, each possessing inherent dignity and worth.

Pastor Sarah Johnson of Grace Community Church shares her experience grappling with this issue: "When we first implemented an AI-powered system to help with pastoral care, I worried we might lose the personal touch that's so crucial in ministry. We had to constantly remind ourselves that these tools are meant to enhance, not replace, human connection."

To address this concern, churches must establish clear guidelines for the use of artificial intelligence in pastoral care and community outreach. These guidelines emphasize the primacy of human interaction and the use of AI as a supportive tool rather than a replacement for personal ministry.

Another significant ethical consideration is the issue of privacy and data security. Artificial intelligence systems often rely on vast amounts of personal data to function effectively. In a ministry context, this data can be particularly sensitive, including information about individuals' spiritual journeys, personal struggles, and financial contributions.

The biblical principle of stewardship extends to the care of this information. As Proverbs 11:13 reminds us, "A gossip betrays a confidence, but a trustworthy person keeps a secret." Churches must treat the data entrusted to them with the utmost respect and implement robust security measures to protect it.

Dr. Michael Chen, a Christian ethicist specializing in technology, emphasizes this point: "When a church member shares personal information, they're not just inputting data into a system. They're entrusting part of their spiritual journey to the church. We have a sacred duty to protect that trust."

Transparency is key in addressing these privacy concerns. Churches should be open about how they collect, use, and protect data. Members should be given clear information about what data is being collected and how it will be used, with the option to opt out of data collection if they choose.

The potential for bias in artificial intelligence systems presents another ethical challenge. These systems inadvertently perpetuate or even amplify existing biases, potentially leading to unfair treatment or discrimination. This is particularly concerning in a church context, where treating everyone as equally important is a fundamental value.

Reverend Thomas Baker of New Life Baptist Church shares his experience: "We were excited about using AI to help tailor our outreach efforts. But we quickly realized we needed to be vigilant about checking for bias. We found that the system was inadvertently favoring certain demographic groups in its recommendations, which went against our mission of being a church for all people."

Addressing this issue requires ongoing vigilance and a commitment to eliminating biases in both the development and implementation of AI systems. Churches should regularly audit their AI tools for bias and ensure that diverse perspectives are included in AI use decision-making processes.

The question of accountability also looms large in the ethical considerations surrounding artificial intelligence. Who is responsible for the outcomes when decisions are increasingly made or influenced by AI systems? This question becomes particularly poignant in a ministry context, where decisions can have profound spiritual and personal implications.

John Stott's words offer guidance here: "Christian leaders are not only responsible for their own lives, but are also shepherds responsible for their flock." This responsibility extends to the implementation and oversight of AI systems in ministry. Church leaders must maintain ultimate accountability for decisions made using AI tools, ensuring that these decisions align with the church's mission and values.

The ethical use of artificial intelligence in ministry also requires addressing the digital divide. As churches increasingly rely on advanced technologies, there's a risk of excluding those who lack access to or familiarity with these tools. This goes against the Christian's call to minister to all.

Pastor Maria Rodriguez of a small rural church expresses her concern: "We serve a community where many people don't have reliable internet access, let alone smartphones. How can we use AI in our ministry without leaving these members behind?"

Addressing this challenge requires a thoughtful approach that balances technological innovation with traditional forms of ministry. Churches must ensure that AI-enhanced services and programs complement, rather than replace, in-person ministry and outreach.

The ethical framework for artificial intelligence in ministry must also grapple with deeper theological questions. Can an AI system truly understand and apply the nuances of Scripture and theology? How do we ensure that AI-powered tools align with our doctrinal positions?

G.K. Chesterton's insight is pertinent here: "The Christian ideal has not been tried and found wanting. It has been found difficult; and left untried." The same could be said for the ethical use of AI in ministry. It's not impossible, but it requires diligence, wisdom, and a commitment to our core values.

Churches should establish clear doctrinal guidelines for their AI systems to address these theological concerns. Qualified spiritual leaders should review and approve all content and recommendations generated by AI to ensure alignment with the church's beliefs and teachings.

As we navigate these ethical considerations, it's crucial to remember that the goal of using artificial intelligence in ministry is not to replace human spiritual leadership, but to enhance our ability to serve God and our communities. AI should be seen as a tool to amplify our capacity for compassion, understanding, and outreach.

In conclusion, the ethical use of artificial intelligence in ministry requires a delicate balance. We must harness this technology's potential to enhance our ministry efforts while steadfastly upholding our Christian values and the primacy of human connection in spiritual growth.

Looking ahead to the next section, we'll explore how these ethical considerations can be practically applied in various ministry contexts. We'll examine case studies of churches that have successfully navigated these ethical challenges, providing concrete examples and strategies for implementing AI in a way that aligns with Christian principles and enhances, rather than detracts from, the core mission of the church.

Section 5.3: Balancing Faith and Innovation

The delicate dance between faith and innovation has been a hallmark of Christianity since its inception. From the early church's use of Roman roads to spread the Gospel to the revolutionary impact of the printing press on Bible distribution, believers have often been at the forefront of adopting new technologies to further God's kingdom. Today, artificial intelligence presents a similar opportunity and challenge. The question is no longer whether to embrace this powerful tool but how to do so while remaining true to timeless faith principles.

C.S. Lewis, in his essay "God in the Dock," penned a thought-provoking statement: "There are no ordinary people. You have never talked to a mere mortal." This profound insight serves as a crucial reminder of the eternal significance of every human interaction. In the age of artificial intelligence, where automation and efficiency often take center stage, Lewis's words call us back to the irreplaceable value of human connection in ministry.

Pastor Sarah's approach to sermon preparation offers a practical example of balancing faith and innovation. She employs an artificial intelligence system to analyze sermon feedback and engagement data. However, rather than allowing the AI to dictate her sermon topics, Sarah uses these insights as one input among many. Her process still prioritizes prayer, in-depth biblical study, and personal discernment. This method demonstrates how technology can enhance, rather than replace, the spiritual aspects of ministry.

John Stott, in his book "The Contemporary Christian," emphasizes the importance of being "contemporary" without becoming "conformist." This principle is particularly relevant when integrating artificial intelligence into ministry. The goal should be to adopt new technologies that enhance our ability to serve and reach people, without compromising core values and beliefs. It's a tightrope walk that requires constant vigilance and discernment.

Pastoral care presents another arena where the balance between faith and innovation is crucial. While artificial intelligence can provide valuable support in areas like scheduling, follow-up reminders, and initial triage of pastoral needs, it should never fully supplant human-to-human pastoral interaction. The warmth of a pastor's smile, the compassion in their voice, and the Spirit-led discernment they bring to a conversation are irreplaceable elements of ministry that no algorithm can replicate.

Once again, G.K. Chesterton's famous quip, "The Christian ideal has not been tried and found wanting. It has been found difficult; and left untried," applies aptly to the challenge of integrating artificial intelligence into ministry. It's tempting to either wholesale reject new technology or uncritically embrace it. The difficult but rewarding path lies in thoughtfully integrating AI in ways that amplify our ability to live out Christian ideals.

A mid-sized church in the Midwest provides an instructive example of this balanced approach. They implemented an artificial intelligence-powered system to identify members who hadn't attended in several weeks. Instead of automatically sending out generic "we miss you" messages, the church used this information to prompt personal outreach from ministry leaders. This strategy effectively balanced the efficiency of AI with the personal touch that is so central to the Christian community.

Bill Scheidler, in his book "The Local Church Today," emphasizes the importance of every-member ministry. He writes, "God's plan for the local church is that every member be a minister." This principle should guide our integration of artificial intelligence into church operations. The goal should not be to create a technocratic elite within our congregations, but to find ways that AI can empower more members to engage in ministry. This might involve using AI to free up time from administrative tasks or providing tools that make certain ministries more accessible to a broader range of people.

One powerful lens through which to view our engagement with artificial intelligence is that of stewardship. The parable of the talents (Matthew

25:14-30) teaches about the importance of wisely using the resources we've been given. Artificial intelligence can be seen as a modern-day "talent" - a powerful resource that we're called to use wisely and fruitfully for God's kingdom. This perspective shifts the question from "Should we use AI?" to "How can we use AI most effectively for God's glory?"

A.W. Tozer, in his spiritual classic "The Pursuit of God," wrote, "What comes into our minds when we think about God is the most important thing about us." As we navigate the integration of artificial intelligence into our ministries, this principle should serve as our north star. Every decision about how to use AI should be filtered through our understanding of God's character and His desires for His church. This approach ensures that our use of technology remains anchored in our faith, rather than drifting into mere efficiency or novelty.

Balancing faith and innovation also means being willing to set boundaries. The capability to use artificial intelligence for a particular task doesn't necessarily mean it's appropriate or beneficial to do so. For instance, while AI could theoretically write entire sermons, most would agree that this crosses an ethical and spiritual line. The process of wrestling with Scripture, seeking God's guidance, and crafting a message for a specific congregation is a deeply spiritual practice that shouldn't be outsourced to an algorithm.

Consider the experience of Pastor David, who leads a growing church in a tech-savvy urban area. Excited by the possibilities of AI, he initially implemented it in nearly every aspect of church operations, from automated email responses to AI-generated social media content. However, he soon noticed a decline in the personal connections that had once characterized his congregation. After much prayer and reflection, David decided to scale back the use of AI in direct communication, reserving it primarily for backend operations and data analysis. This allowed him to leverage the efficiency of AI while preserving the human touch in member interactions.

The challenge of balancing faith and innovation extends beyond the walls of the church. As artificial intelligence becomes more prevalent in society, pastors and church leaders have a responsibility to help their congregations navigate its use in their daily lives. This might involve teaching on the ethical use of technology, offering workshops on digital discipleship, or providing guidance on maintaining authentic relationships in an increasingly digital world.

In his book, Every Good Endeavor, Dr. Timothy Keller discusses the importance of seeing our work as a calling from God. This principle can be extended to our use of technology in ministry. When we view the integration of artificial intelligence into our churches as part of our calling—a way to more effectively fulfill the Great Commission—it transforms it from a mere technological upgrade to a spiritual endeavor.

As we conclude this exploration of balancing faith and innovation, it's clear that there are no easy answers or one-size-fits-all solutions. Each church and ministry must prayerfully consider how to integrate artificial intelligence in a way that aligns with their specific calling and context. However, we can navigate this new terrain faithfully by grounding ourselves in biblical principles, learning from the wisdom of Christian thinkers past and present, and approaching these challenges with prayer and discernment.

The journey of balancing faith and innovation is ongoing. As artificial intelligence continues to evolve, so too must our approach to its use in ministry. This requires a commitment to lifelong learning, not just about technology, but about how to apply timeless biblical truths to new contexts.

In the next chapter, we'll delve into practical applications of artificial intelligence in various aspects of ministry, from sermon preparation to pastoral care. We'll explore real-world examples of how churches are putting these principles into practice, reaping the benefits of AI while staying true to their calling as shepherds of God's flock. As we move forward, let's keep in mind the words of the Apostle Paul in 1 Corinthians 10:31: "So whether you eat or drink or whatever you do, do it all for the glory of God." May our use of artificial intelligence in ministry always be guided by this ultimate purpose, balancing the best human innovation with our faith's timeless truths.

CHAPTER SIX

The Role of AI in Modern Ministry

Section 6.1: How AI is Shaping Ministry Today

In the landscape of modern ministry, artificial intelligence has emerged as a transformative force, reshaping the ways we serve, teach, and connect with our congregations. This technological revolution isn't about replacing the human touch in ministry; rather, it's about enhancing and extending our capabilities to reach more people with the Gospel message in increasingly effective and personalized ways.

Consider the story of Pastor James, who leads a small church in rural America. For years, he struggled to maintain consistent communication with his congregation, especially the younger members, who seemed to drift away. The introduction of artificial intelligence-powered tools into his ministry changed everything. Now, Pastor James uses a smart scheduling system that not only reminds him of important dates like birthdays and anniversaries but also suggests personalized messages to send to each member. This simple yet effective use of artificial intelligence has dramatically improved his ability to stay connected with his flock, making each person feel valued and remembered.

"I used to spend hours trying to keep track of everyone's important life events," Pastor James recalls. "Now, with this AI-powered system, I can focus on crafting meaningful messages and prayers for each person, knowing I won't miss anyone's special day. It's like having a tireless assistant who knows my congregation as well as I do."

The influence of artificial intelligence in ministry extends far beyond administrative tasks. It's revolutionizing how pastors approach Bible study and sermon preparation. Advanced language models can now analyze vast amounts of theological texts, providing insights and connections that might have otherwise been missed. This doesn't replace the pastor's role in studying and interpreting Scripture, but it does provide a powerful tool to enhance their understanding and ability to communicate God's Word effectively.

Take, for instance, the experience of Reverend Sarah, who leads a thriving urban congregation. She uses an artificial intelligence-powered Bible study tool that helps her explore the original Greek and Hebrew texts, providing nuanced interpretations and cross-references. This deep dive into Scripture, aided by artificial intelligence, has enriched her sermons and Bible studies, allowing her to present the Word with greater depth and clarity.

"It's like having a team of scholars at my fingertips," Reverend Sarah explains. "The AI tool helps me uncover layers of meaning in the text that I might have overlooked. It's particularly helpful when I'm preparing sermons on complex passages or addressing difficult questions from my congregation."

Artificial intelligence is also revolutionizing outreach and evangelism efforts. Churches are now able to analyze data on community needs and tailor their outreach programs accordingly. A church in a college town used artificial intelligence to analyze local demographic data and social media trends. They discovered a significant population of international students feeling isolated and homesick. In response, they launched a targeted ministry program offering language exchange, cultural events, and support groups, effectively reaching a segment of their community they had previously overlooked.

The impact of this data-driven approach was profound. Within six months, the church saw a 30% increase in attendance from international students, and several new small groups were formed specifically to address this community's unique needs. The church's outreach director, Mark, notes, "Without the insights provided by AI, we might never have realized the opportunity we had to serve this group. It's opened our eyes to needs in our community we didn't even know existed."

Moreover, artificial intelligence is enhancing accessibility in worship. Churches are using real-time translation services powered by artificial intelligence to make their services accessible to non-native speakers. Closed captioning generated by artificial intelligence is helping the hearing-impaired engage more fully in services. These technological advancements are breaking down barriers and making the church more inclusive than ever before.

At Cornerstone Community Church, the implementation of AI-powered translation services has transformed their multilingual congregation. Pastor Lee shares, "We have members from over 20 different countries. Before, we struggled to provide translation for everyone. Now, with AI, each person can hear the sermon in their native language. It's like a modern-day Pentecost miracle every Sunday!"

The renowned Christian apologist C.S. Lewis once wrote, "God cannot give us a happiness and peace apart from Himself, because it is not there. There is no such thing." This profound truth reminds us that while artificial intelligence provides powerful tools, it is merely a means to an end – that end being a deeper connection with God and His people. The goal of integrating artificial intelligence into ministry should always be to bring people closer to Christ and to facilitate a more profound understanding of His Word.

Artificial intelligence is also making waves in pastoral care. Many churches are implementing chatbots that can provide immediate support and resources to members in need. These AI-driven assistants can offer prayer suggestions, scripture references for comfort, and even direct individuals to appropriate mental health resources when necessary. While they don't replace the need for human pastoral care, they provide an additional layer of support, especially during times when human pastors may not be immediately available.

Grace Baptist Church in rural Kentucky implemented an AI chatbot named "Grace" to supplement their pastoral care efforts. Deacon John Wilkins explains, "Grace doesn't replace human interaction, but it provides immediate support when someone is struggling at 2 AM and needs a word of encouragement. It's been especially helpful for our younger members who are more comfortable texting than calling."

Since implementing Grace, the church has seen a 30% reduction in non-emergency calls to pastoral staff, allowing them to focus on more critical care needs. Additionally, they've noticed an uptick in younger members seeking pastoral counseling, often prompted by initial interactions with the chatbot.

In the realm of church administration, artificial intelligence is streamlining operations and freeing up valuable time for ministry leaders. From automated bookkeeping systems to smart donation platforms, these tools are reducing the administrative burden on church staff. This allows pastors and leaders to focus more on their core mission of shepherding their flock and spreading the Gospel.

Pastor Tom of Hillside Community Church shares his experience: "Before we implemented AI-powered administrative tools, I spent at least 15 hours a week on paperwork and financial management. Now, that's down to about 5 hours. Those extra 10 hours a week have allowed me to start a new discipleship program and spend more one-on-one time with church members who need support."

The impact of artificial intelligence on youth ministry is particularly noteworthy. Many churches are using AI-powered apps and platforms to engage young people in Bible study and discipleship. These tools use gamification and personalized learning paths to make spiritual growth more engaging and interactive for tech-savvy youth.

Youth pastor Rachel at New Life Church has seen remarkable results with an AI-driven Bible study app. "Our teens are glued to their phones anyway, so we decided to meet them where they are," she says. "The app uses AI to tailor Bible study plans to each user's interests and learning style. We've seen a 50% increase in daily Bible reading among our youth group since we introduced it."

As we witness these transformations, it's crucial to remember the words of John Stott, who said, "We must be global Christians with a global vision because our God is a global God." Artificial intelligence is enabling churches to expand their global vision, reaching across language barriers and geographical boundaries to spread the message of Christ.

This global reach is exemplified by Online Mission Church, a digital-first ministry that uses AI to connect with seekers worldwide. Pastor David explains, "Our AI system helps us identify people searching online for answers to spiritual questions. We can then reach out with relevant content and offer personal connections. We've had people from over 100 countries engage with our ministry in the past year alone."

However, as we embrace these technological advancements, we must also be mindful of potential pitfalls. The efficiency of AI systems might tempt church leaders to rely too heavily on automated processes, potentially losing the personal touch that is so crucial in pastoral care.

Looking ahead, the potential for artificial intelligence in ministry seems boundless. From AI-assisted counseling to virtual reality Bible experiences, the future holds exciting possibilities for how we can use technology to deepen faith and build community.

In the following sections, we'll delve deeper into specific case studies that illustrate how churches are practically implementing artificial intelligence in their ministries. We'll also discuss the potential challenges and ethical considerations that arise from this technological integration in greater detail.

Section 6.2: Case Studies: AI in Action in Churches

To truly grasp the transformative power of artificial intelligence in ministry, examining real-world examples of churches harnessing this technology to enhance their mission and reach proves invaluable. These case studies illustrate the diverse ways artificial intelligence can amplify the church's ability to fulfill its mission, from personalizing spiritual growth to expanding pastoral care and refining community outreach.

Hillside Community Church: Personalized Spiritual Growth Plans

Hillside Community Church, a mid-sized congregation in suburban Seattle, implemented an artificial intelligence-driven spiritual growth platform. This system analyzes members' engagement with church activities, their responses to biblical questions, and their personal goals to create tailored spiritual development plans.

223

Pastor Mark Thompson explains, "The artificial intelligence system helps us understand where each member is in their faith journey. It suggests relevant Bible studies, volunteer opportunities, and even potential mentors within our congregation. It's like having a personal spiritual advisor for each of our 500 members."

The results have been remarkable. Church engagement increased by 40%, and the number of members involved in small groups doubled. One member, Sarah Chen, shared, "The personalized recommendations helped me find a Bible study group that perfectly aligned with my current spiritual questions. I feel more connected to God and my church family than ever before."

The system's success lies in its ability to recognize patterns and make connections that might escape human observation. For instance, it noticed that members who attended a specific financial stewardship class were more likely to increase their involvement in community service. This insight led to the creation of a new program that combined financial wisdom with outreach opportunities, further strengthening the church's impact on the community.

Pastor Thompson adds, "We've always believed in meeting people where they are in their spiritual journey. This AI system helps us do that more effectively than we ever could manually. It's not about replacing personal connections, but about enhancing them and ensuring no one falls through the cracks."

Grace Baptist Church: Enhancing Pastoral Care

In rural Kentucky, Grace Baptist Church faced a challenge common to many small churches - providing comprehensive pastoral care with limited staff. They turned to an artificial intelligence-powered chatbot to supplement their care efforts.

The chatbot, affectionately named "Grace," is available 24/7 to answer basic questions about faith, provide comforting scripture verses, and even offer simple prayer guidance. For more complex issues, Grace directs members to appropriate human staff or resources.

One unexpected benefit emerged when Grace identified a trend in late-night conversations about loneliness among elderly members. This insight led to the creation of a new ministry focused on combating isolation in the senior community.

"We never realized how many of our older members were up late, feeling alone," says Pastor Robert Lee. "Grace not only provided them comfort in the moment but helped us see a need we were missing. Now we have a thriving senior fellowship program that meets in the evenings."

Lighthouse Fellowship: Revolutionizing Community Outreach

Lighthouse Fellowship, an urban church in Chicago, employed artificial intelligence to revolutionize their community outreach efforts. They used advanced data analysis to identify unmet needs in their neighborhood and tailor their programs accordingly.

The artificial intelligence system analyzed public data on poverty rates, education levels, and health statistics, combined with social media sentiment analysis about community issues. This led to the creation of targeted initiatives, including a job skills training program, a mental health support group, and a literacy program for adults.

Outreach Director Maria Gonzales shares, "The artificial intelligence showed us needs we hadn't even considered. We discovered a large population of single fathers struggling to balance work and childcare. In response, we started a support group and childcare program specifically for them."

Within a year of implementing these data-driven initiatives, Lighthouse Fellowship saw a 50% increase in community engagement and a 25% growth in church attendance.

The AI system also helped the church optimize its resource allocation. Analyzing patterns in program attendance and outcomes suggested shifting resources from less effective programs to those with higher impact. This data-driven approach allowed the church to maximize its community impact with limited resources.

Pastor David Chen reflects, "As shepherds, we're called to know our flock. In today's complex urban environment, AI helps us understand our community in ways we never could before. It's like having a bird's eye view of our neighborhood's needs, allowing us to be more strategic and effective in our outreach."

New Life Church: Engaging Youth Through Technology

New Life Church, a large congregation in Texas, faced declining youth engagement. They turned to artificial intelligence to create an interactive, personalized discipleship program for their younger members.

The church developed an AI-powered app that gamifies Bible study and spiritual disciplines. The app uses machine learning to adapt to each user's learning style, interests, and spiritual maturity level, creating personalized daily challenges and study plans.

Youth Pastor Sarah Martinez explains, "The app might challenge one teen to memorize a verse, another to journal about a specific topic, and another to perform an act of service - all based on their individual spiritual journeys and learning preferences."

The results were impressive. Within six months, daily app engagement reached 80% among the youth group members. Bible literacy scores improved by 35%, and youth service participation increased by 50%.

One unexpected outcome was the app's ability to flag potential issues. When a user's engagement pattern suddenly changed, or their responses indicated potential struggles, the system alerted youth leaders, allowing for timely pastoral intervention.

"The AI doesn't replace our role as mentors," Pastor Martinez emphasizes. "Instead, it enhances our ability to guide and support our youth. It's like having a 24/7 pulse on their spiritual health."

These case studies illustrate the diverse and powerful ways artificial intelligence can enhance ministry. From personalizing spiritual growth to expanding pastoral care and refining community outreach, AI is proving to be a valuable tool in the modern church's mission to spread the Gospel and nurture faith.

As we reflect on these examples, the words of C.S. Lewis come to mind: "God whispers to us in our pleasures, speaks in our conscience, but shouts in our pains: it is His megaphone to rouse a deaf world." Perhaps in our technological age, artificial intelligence can serve as another channel through which God's message can reach His people, amplifying the church's ability to hear the whispers, speak to the conscience, and respond to the pain in our communities.

In the next section, we'll explore the potential challenges and ethical considerations that arise as we integrate artificial intelligence into our ministries. While the benefits are clear, it's crucial that we approach this powerful tool with wisdom, discernment, and a firm grounding in our faith and values.

Section 6.3: Potential Challenges and Ethical Considerations

While the benefits of artificial intelligence in ministry are evident, approaching this technology with discernment and wisdom is crucial. As stewards of both our congregations and the Gospel message, carefully considering the challenges and ethical implications that arise from integrating artificial intelligence into our ministries becomes paramount.

Data Privacy and Security

One of the primary concerns when using artificial intelligence in ministry is the protection of personal data. Churches often handle sensitive information

231

about their members, including personal struggles, financial contributions, and spiritual journeys. The use of artificial intelligence systems to process and analyze this data raises important questions about privacy and security.

Dr. Elizabeth Watkins, a Christian ethicist specializing in technology, warns, "Churches must be vigilant in protecting their members' data. The trust between a pastor and their congregation is sacred, and that trust extends to how we handle digital information."

Churches implementing artificial intelligence systems need to ensure robust data protection measures are in place. This includes using secure, encrypted systems, regularly updating security protocols, and being transparent with congregation members about how their data is used and protected.

Pastor John Richards of Faith Community Church shares his experience: "When we first introduced AI-powered tools, some members were concerned about their privacy. We held town hall meetings to explain our data policies and security measures. We also appointed a data protection officer from within our congregation to oversee these efforts. It's all about maintaining trust."

The Risk of Depersonalization

While artificial intelligence can enhance personalization in many ways, there's also a risk of inadvertently depersonalizing ministry. The efficiency of artificial intelligence systems might tempt church leaders to rely too heavily on automated processes, potentially losing the personal touch that is so crucial in pastoral care.

Reverend Thomas Baker of Grace Episcopal Church cautions, "We must remember that AI is a tool, not a replacement for human connection. The danger lies in becoming overly reliant on technology and losing sight of the relational aspect of ministry."

To mitigate this risk, churches should establish clear guidelines for when and how artificial intelligence tools are used in pastoral care. For instance, AI chatbots might be useful for initial contact or providing basic information but should always have a clear pathway to human interaction for more complex or sensitive issues.

Ethical Use of Predictive Analytics

Artificial intelligence's ability to predict behavior based on data analysis raises ethical questions. While this capability can be used to identify members who might be drifting away from the church or those in need of specific support, it also treads a fine line between pastoral care and invasion of privacy.

Dr. Michael Thornton, a theologian focusing on the intersection of faith and technology, points out,

"There's a delicate balance between using data to serve our congregation better and respecting individual autonomy. We must ask ourselves: At what point does predictive analytics become manipulative or coercive?"

Churches using such systems should be transparent about their use and give members the option to opt-out. Moreover, any insights gained through AI analysis should be used as a starting point for personal outreach, not as a definitive judgment.

The Challenge of Algorithmic Bias

Artificial intelligence systems can inadvertently perpetuate or even amplify existing biases. This is particularly concerning in a church context "If we're not careful, AI systems could reinforce cultural or racial biases in our ministry approaches," warns Dr. Lydia Chen, a computer scientist and active church member. "For example, an AI system might suggest different outreach strategies based on demographic data, potentially leading to unintended discrimination."

To address this, churches should regularly audit their AI systems for bias and ensure diverse representation in the teams overseeing AI implementation. It's also crucial to combine AI insights with human wisdom and discernment.

Maintaining the Human Element in Spiritual Growth

While artificial intelligence can provide valuable insights and personalized recommendations for spiritual growth, there's a risk of over-relying on technology in an inherently personal and spiritual process.

Reverend Sarah Johnson of New Life Community Church shares, "We found that some members were becoming more focused on completing AI-suggested tasks than on genuine spiritual reflection. We had to recalibrate our approach to emphasize that these tools are aids to, not substitutes for, personal spiritual disciplines and community engagement."

Churches should strive to maintain a balance, using AI to support and enhance spiritual growth initiatives while emphasizing the irreplaceable value of personal prayer, reflection, and community fellowship.

Theological Implications

The use of artificial intelligence in ministry also raises deeper theological questions. Can a machine-learning algorithm truly understand and apply the nuances of Scripture and theology? How do we ensure that AI-powered tools align with our church's doctrinal positions?

Theologian Dr. Robert Thompson reflects, "We must remember that AI, no matter how advanced, lacks the spirit of discernment that comes from the Holy Spirit. It can be a powerful tool for organizing and analyzing information, but the interpretation and application of Scripture must remain in human hands, guided by the Spirit."

Churches should establish clear theological guidelines for their AI systems and ensure that all content and recommendations are reviewed by qualified spiritual leaders.

Resource Allocation and the Digital Divide

Implementing advanced AI systems requires significant resources, both in terms of finances and technical expertise. This raises concerns about creating a digital divide between churches that can afford such technologies and those that cannot.

Pastor Maria Gonzales of a small rural church expresses her concern: "We barely have enough in our budget for basic operations. How can we keep up with larger churches using these advanced AI tools? I worry about our ability to serve our community effectively in this digital age."

Addressing this challenge may require denominational bodies or Christian tech organizations to develop affordable, scalable AI solutions that can be implemented by churches of all sizes and resource levels.

As we navigate these challenges, the words of the apostle Paul in 1 Corinthians 10:23 offer guidance: "'I have the right to do anything,' you say—but not everything is beneficial. 'I have the right to do anything'—but not everything is constructive." This principle applies aptly to our use of artificial intelligence in ministry. While we have the capability to implement these powerful tools, we must carefully consider whether and how their use truly benefits our ministry and constructively serves our mission to share the love of Christ.

In conclusion, the integration of artificial intelligence into ministry presents both exciting opportunities and significant challenges. As church leaders, we are called to approach these technologies with wisdom, ethical consideration, and always with an eye towards fulfilling our primary mission of sharing the Gospel and nurturing faith.

Looking ahead to the next chapter, we'll explore practical strategies for implementing artificial intelligence in your church. We'll discuss how to assess your ministry's needs, choose appropriate AI tools, and develop a roadmap for integration that aligns with your church's values and mission. By thoughtfully navigating the path ahead, we can harness the power of artificial intelligence to enhance our ministries while staying true to our calling as shepherds of God's flock.

PART TWO

PART II: Practical Applications of AI in Ministry

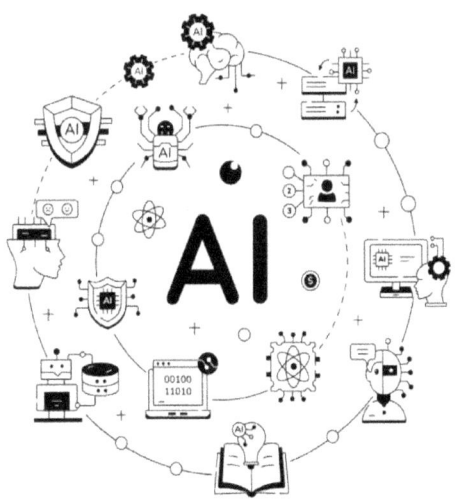

CHAPTER SEVEN

AI for Sermon Preparation

Section 7.1: Using AI for Biblical Research and Exegesis

To build on our exploration of artificial intelligence in biblical research and exegesis, let's consider how these tools can enhance our study of biblical languages. For many pastors, the nuances of Hebrew and Greek can be challenging to navigate, especially years after any formal training. Artificial intelligence-powered language tools can bridge this gap, offering instant analysis of word roots, grammatical structures, and semantic ranges.

Take, for example, the study of the word "chesed" in the Old Testament. This rich Hebrew term, often translated as "lovingkindness" or "steadfast love," carries deep theological significance. An artificial intelligence tool could provide a comprehensive overview of its usage across the Old Testament, highlighting nuances in different contexts. It might reveal how the term is used in covenantal language, in descriptions of God's character, and in human relationships. This depth of understanding can transform a sermon on God's love from a general exposition to a rich, multi-layered exploration of divine faithfulness.

G.K. Chesterton once wrote, "The Bible tells us to love our neighbors, and also to love our enemies; probably because they are generally the same people." Artificial intelligence can help us unpack such paradoxes by providing cultural and historical context. When studying Jesus' command to love our enemies, an artificial intelligence tool could offer insights into the political and social tensions of first-century Palestine, the Roman occupation, and the Jewish expectations of the Messiah. This contextual understanding can help us apply these challenging teachings to our modern world with greater clarity and relevance.

However, as we leverage these powerful tools, we must remain vigilant against the temptation to rely solely on technology. John Stott wisely cautioned, "Knowledge is indispensable to Christian life and service. If we do not use the mind which God has given us, we condemn ourselves to spiritual superficiality." Artificial intelligence should enhance, not replace, our critical thinking and spiritual discernment.

One of the most exciting applications of artificial intelligence in biblical research is its ability to identify thematic connections across Scripture. This capability can be particularly valuable when preparing topical sermons or studying biblical theology. For instance, if you're preparing a series on the concept of redemption, an artificial intelligence tool could trace this theme from Genesis to Revelation, highlighting key passages, recurring motifs, and the progressive revelation of God's redemptive plan.

Imagine exploring how the Exodus narrative prefigures Christ's redemptive work, or how the kinsman-redeemer in Ruth points to Jesus' role as our Redeemer. Artificial intelligence can quickly identify these connections, providing a rich tapestry of biblical imagery and theology to inform your preaching. This comprehensive view of Scripture aligns with the words of Jesus in Luke 24:27, "And beginning with Moses and all the Prophets, he explained to them what was said in all the Scriptures concerning himself."

Artificial intelligence can also assist in analyzing the literary structures and genres of biblical texts. Understanding whether a passage is narrative, poetry, prophecy, or epistle is crucial for proper interpretation. Advanced algorithms can identify literary techniques, parallelisms, and other literary devices that might not be immediately apparent, especially in translation. This literary analysis can enhance our appreciation of the Bible not just as a theological text, but as a masterpiece of divine communication.

For instance, when studying the book of Amos, an artificial intelligence tool might highlight the prophet's use of repetition, irony, and vivid imagery. It could draw parallels between Amos's rhetorical style and other prophetic books, enriching our understanding of prophetic literature as a whole. This deeper appreciation of biblical genres can help us communicate the power and beauty of God's Word more effectively to our congregations.

As we harness these tools, we must remember the words of A.W. Tozer: "The Bible is not an end in itself, but a means to bring men to an intimate and satisfying knowledge of God." Our goal in using artificial intelligence for biblical research and exegesis should always be to draw closer to God and to help our congregations do the same.

Artificial intelligence can also aid in cross-referencing and intertextual analysis. The New Testament frequently quotes or alludes to the Old Testament, and understanding these connections is crucial for sound biblical interpretation. An artificial intelligence tool could quickly identify all the Old Testament references in a New Testament passage, providing context and explaining how the New Testament authors interpreted and applied these texts.

For example, when preparing a sermon on Romans 3, an artificial intelligence tool could highlight Paul's use of Old Testament quotations, explain their original context, and show how Paul applies them to his argument about justification by faith. This comprehensive view can help us preach with greater depth and authority, showing the unity and coherence of God's revelation across both testaments.

Another valuable application of artificial intelligence in biblical research is in the area of word studies. While concordances have long been a staple of pastoral study, artificial intelligence takes this to a new level. Not only can it provide exhaustive lists of where a word appears in Scripture, but it can also analyze the context of each usage, identify patterns, and even suggest related concepts or synonyms.

Consider a study of the concept of "joy" in the Bible. An artificial intelligence tool could quickly show how this concept is expressed across different biblical genres, from the Psalms to the Gospels to the Epistles. It might reveal that joy is often associated with God's presence, with obedience, or with future hope. This comprehensive view can add depth and richness to our preaching on such themes.

Artificial intelligence can also assist in analyzing the historical and cultural background of biblical texts. By cross-referencing biblical content with historical databases, these tools can provide valuable insights into the social, political, and religious context of various passages. This can be particularly helpful when dealing with passages that might seem obscure or difficult to modern readers.

For instance, when studying Jesus' interactions with the Pharisees, an artificial intelligence tool could provide a detailed overview of first-century Jewish sects, their beliefs and practices, and the political tensions of the time. This background information can help us and our congregations better understand the radical nature of Jesus' teachings and actions in their original context.

As we leverage these powerful tools, we must always remember that our ultimate goal is not just to accumulate knowledge, but to grow in our relationship with God and to help others do the same. As Oswald Chambers wrote, "The purpose of Bible study is not to know the Bible, but to know God through the Bible." Artificial intelligence should serve this purpose, enhancing our ability to understand and communicate God's truth, not replacing our dependence on the Holy Spirit for illumination and application.

Furthermore, artificial intelligence can assist in identifying contemporary applications of biblical principles. These tools can suggest ways to bridge the gap between ancient texts and modern life by analyzing current events, social trends, and even local community data. This can be particularly valuable when preparing sermons that speak directly to the challenges and questions facing our congregations.

For example, when preparing a sermon series on the Ten Commandments, an artificial intelligence tool could not only provide comprehensive biblical and theological resources on each commandment but also suggest contemporary issues where these ancient laws might offer guidance. It might highlight how the commandment against stealing relates to modern issues of digital piracy or corporate ethics or how the commandment to honor one's parents might apply in an age of increasing eldercare challenges.

However, as we embrace these technological aids, we must heed the warning of Ravi Zacharias: "We have moved from a society where people looked to God for answers to one where people look to technology for answers." Our use of artificial intelligence in sermon preparation should always point people back to God, not to technology itself.

In conclusion, artificial intelligence offers unprecedented opportunities to enhance our biblical research and exegesis. From deep language analysis to thematic studies, from historical context to contemporary application, these tools can significantly expand our capacity for in-depth study of God's Word. However, they remain tools, not replacements for the pastor's role in prayerfully studying and applying Scripture.

As we move forward into this new era of sermon preparation, let us hold fast to the words of Paul in 2 Timothy 2:15, "Do your best to present yourself to God as one approved, a worker who does not need to be ashamed and who correctly handles the word of truth." May our use of artificial intelligence in biblical research and exegesis always serve this higher purpose, equipping us to more faithfully and effectively proclaim God's truth in our rapidly changing world.

Section 7.2: AI Tools for Sermon Writing

The art of crafting a sermon is as old as the Christian faith itself, yet in our rapidly evolving digital age, pastors now have access to tools that would have seemed like science fiction just a few decades ago. Artificial intelligence stands at the forefront of this technological revolution, offering innovative ways to enhance the sermon writing process. However, it's crucial to approach these new tools with wisdom and discernment, ensuring they serve to amplify, not replace, the God-given gifts of insight and inspiration.

Picture yourself sitting at your desk, the Bible open, notes scattered around, and the blank page of your sermon document staring back at you. The weight of Sunday morning looms, and you're seeking the right words to bring God's truth to life for your congregation. This is where artificial intelligence can step in as a valuable assistant, not to write the sermon for you but to help unlock your creativity and streamline your process.

One of the primary ways artificial intelligence aids in sermon writing is through advanced language models. These sophisticated systems can generate outlines, suggest illustrations, and even draft portions of sermons based on inputted themes or Scripture passages. However, it's vital to view these outputs as starting points rather than finished products.

Imagine you're preparing a sermon series on the Beatitudes. You input Matthew 5:3-12 into an artificial intelligence tool, along with your initial thoughts and study notes. Within moments, the system might generate a structured outline, complete with potential main points, sub-points, and even suggested illustrations for each Beatitude. This outline could serve as a springboard for your own creativity, highlighting aspects of the text you hadn't considered or suggesting connections that spark fresh insights.

For instance, artificial intelligence might propose linking the concept of being "poor in spirit" with contemporary issues of materialism and social media-driven self-promotion. It could suggest an illustration comparing the "meek" to unsung heroes in your local community. These ideas can help shape your sermon, but the heart of the message – the unique insight God has laid on your heart for your specific congregation – must come from your own prayerful reflection and pastoral discernment.

As John Stott wisely counseled, "The sermon is not just a piece of rhetoric or a work of art; it is an encounter with the living God." Artificial intelligence can help structure our thoughts and expand our perspectives, but it cannot replicate the profound spiritual experience of wrestling with a text and emerging with a God-given message.

Another valuable application of artificial intelligence in sermon writing is in the realm of language enhancement. Advanced algorithms can analyze your draft, suggesting improvements in clarity, coherence, and impact. They can help identify areas where your argument might be strengthened, where illustrations might be more effectively placed, or where your language could be more engaging.

Let's say you're crafting a sermon on the fruit of the Spirit. You've written your first draft, focusing on the concept of love. An artificial intelligence tool might analyze your text and suggest ways to make your points more memorable. It could recommend using more sensory language to describe God's love, propose a structure that builds to a powerful climax or suggests transitions that more clearly link your points together. These recommendations can help refine your message, making it more accessible and impactful for your listeners.

However, we must be cautious not to let artificial intelligence homogenize our unique voices. As C.S. Lewis noted, "Even in literature and art, no man who bothers about originality will ever be original: whereas if you simply try to tell the truth (without caring twopence how often it has been told before) you will, nine times out of ten, become original without ever having noticed it." Your authentic voice, shaped by your experiences, your relationship with God, and your love for your congregation, is irreplaceable.

Artificial intelligence can also assist in crafting illustrations and applications. By analyzing vast databases of literature, current events, and even local community information, these tools can suggest relevant stories or examples that bring your sermon points to life. This capability can be particularly helpful when addressing complex theological concepts or when seeking to make ancient truths relevant to contemporary life.

Consider a sermon on the concept of covenant faithfulness. An artificial intelligence tool might suggest illustrations from history, literature, or current events that powerfully demonstrate unwavering commitment in the face of adversity. It could propose applications that resonate with different demographics in your congregation, from young professionals to retirees. For example, it might suggest linking the concept of covenant faithfulness to the challenges of maintaining long-term commitments in a culture of instant gratification or to the idea of perseverance in difficult workplace situations.

Yet, as we leverage these tools, we must remember the words of A.W. Tozer: "Truth is a glorious but hard mistress. She never consults, bargains or compromises." While artificial intelligence can help us communicate truth more effectively, it must never lead us to water down or compromise the message of Scripture.

One of the most exciting applications of artificial intelligence in sermon writing is its ability to help tailor messages to specific audiences. By analyzing data on congregation demographics, past sermon feedback, and even community trends, these tools can suggest ways to make your message more relevant and impactful for your particular flock.

For example, if you're preaching on stewardship in a congregation with many young families, an artificial intelligence tool might suggest focusing on long-term financial planning and generosity in the context of raising children. If your congregation includes many retirees, it might propose exploring the concept of legacy giving. This audience-aware approach can help ensure your sermons speak directly to the needs and concerns of your congregation.

However, we must be cautious not to let data-driven insights override the leading of the Holy Spirit. As Oswald Chambers reminds us, "The goal of prayer is not to get man's will done in heaven, but to get God's will done on earth." Our primary guide in sermon preparation must always be God's Word and His Spirit, not algorithms and data analysis.

Artificial intelligence can also assist in the crucial task of sermon editing. Advanced language models can help identify areas where your message might be unclear, repetitive, or off-topic. They can suggest ways to tighten your argument, enhance your transitions, and ensure your conclusion powerfully reinforces your main points.

Imagine you're working on a sermon series on the Lord's Prayer. You've drafted your message on "Give us this day our daily bread," but you're not quite satisfied with how it's coming together. An artificial intelligence tool could analyze your draft and suggest ways to clearly link the concept of daily provision to trust in God's faithfulness. It might recommend restructuring your points for greater impact or proposing a more memorable conclusion. These editing suggestions can be invaluable, especially when time is short and fresh eyes are not available.

In practical terms, integrating artificial intelligence into your sermon writing process might look something like this: After your initial study and prayer, you input your chosen Scripture passage and main ideas into an artificial intelligence tool. You review the generated outline and suggestions, selecting those that resonate with your vision for the sermon. As you write, you periodically run your draft through the tool for language enhancement and structural suggestions. Near the end of your process, you use the tool to help fine-tune your illustrations and applications.

Throughout this process, it's crucial to maintain a posture of discernment and dependence on the Holy Spirit. Artificial intelligence is a tool, not a replacement for your pastoral wisdom and spiritual insight. It's also important to be transparent with your congregation about your use of these tools. This openness can model responsible engagement with technology and demonstrate how new innovations can be used in service of timeless truths.

For those interested in delving deeper into the technical aspects of artificial intelligence in sermon writing, our companion book, "AI for Novices," offers a more detailed exploration of the algorithms and processes involved. However, for most pastors, a basic understanding of these tools' capabilities and limitations is sufficient to harness their benefits effectively.

As we look to the future, artificial intelligence will likely play an increasingly significant role in sermon preparation. However, the essence of preaching – the proclamation of God's truth through a messenger touched by His Spirit – remains unchanged. Artificial intelligence can enhance our ability to craft well-structured, engaging, and relevant sermons, but it can never replace the power of a message born out of a personal encounter with the living God.

In our next exploration, we'll delve into how artificial intelligence can further assist in the crucial final step of sermon preparation: delivery. The journey from page to pulpit presents its own set of challenges and opportunities, and artificial intelligence offers intriguing possibilities for enhancing this vital aspect of preaching ministry...

Section 7.3: Enhancing Sermon Delivery with AI

The journey from crafting a sermon to delivering it effectively is a crucial transition in the preaching process. It's here, in the moment of delivery, that the carefully prepared words come to life, touching hearts and transforming lives. Artificial intelligence, while not the first thing that comes to mind when considering sermon delivery, offers intriguing possibilities for enhancing this vital aspect of preaching ministry.

Imagine standing before your congregation, notes in hand, ready to share the message God has laid on your heart. The weight of responsibility is palpable. In these moments, every tool at our disposal becomes valuable, and artificial intelligence can be one such tool, working behind the scenes to support and enhance your delivery.

One of the primary ways artificial intelligence can aid in sermon delivery is through real-time feedback systems. These advanced tools can analyze various aspects of your delivery - pace, tone, volume, even body language - and provide subtle cues to help you adjust in the moment. For instance, a small device could gently vibrate if your speaking pace becomes too rapid, or a discreet earpiece could remind you to vary your tone for emphasis.

Consider the experience of Pastor James, leader of a growing suburban church. James had always struggled with speaking too quickly when he became passionate about a topic. He decided to try an artificial intelligence-powered feedback system during his sermons. The first Sunday he used it, he was amazed at how the gentle reminders helped him maintain a more measured pace without interrupting his flow of thought. His congregation noticed the difference, commenting on how much easier it was to follow and absorb his message.

However, as we embrace these technological aids, we must heed the warning of John Stott: "Preaching is not a mere human art, but a spiritual exercise which demands the preacher's utmost dependence upon the Holy Spirit." The goal of using artificial intelligence in sermon delivery should always be to remove distractions and enhance communication, not to create a performance or detract from the message itself.

Another fascinating application of artificial intelligence in sermon delivery is in the realm of adaptive presentations. Imagine a system that could detect the engagement levels of your congregation and subtly adjust your prepared slides or visual aids in real-time. If attention seems to be waning, it might suggest moving to a more engaging illustration or highlighting a key point to recapture focus.

For example, Pastor Sarah, known for her dynamic preaching style, incorporated an artificial intelligence system into her sermon presentations. During a message on the parables of Jesus, the system detected a dip in engagement when she began discussing agricultural practices in ancient Israel. It promptly suggested displaying a modern farming analogy she had prepared as a backup, helping to reconnect her urban congregation with the message.

While such tools can be powerful aids, we must remember the words of A.W. Tozer: "The Holy Spirit can never be replaced by technology or human ingenuity." Our primary reliance must always be on the Spirit's guidance and power, with technology serving as a support, not a substitute.

Artificial intelligence can also assist in improving accessibility during sermon delivery. Advanced speech-to-text algorithms can provide real-time captioning for hearing-impaired members of the congregation. Similarly, for multilingual congregations, artificial intelligence-powered translation systems can offer simultaneous interpretation, breaking down language barriers and ensuring the message reaches every member of the flock.

Consider the testimony of Pastor Lee, who leads a diverse congregation in a major metropolitan area. By implementing an artificial intelligence translation system, he was able to preach in English while non-English speaking members received real-time translations through discreet earpieces. The impact was profound, unifying the congregation and allowing everyone to engage with the message simultaneously.

However, as we leverage these tools, we must be mindful of potential pitfalls. The use of technology in worship settings can sometimes become a distraction if not implemented thoughtfully.

In practical terms, integrating artificial intelligence into sermon delivery might involve a period of adjustment and learning. It's crucial to practice with these tools before using them in a live setting, ensuring they enhance rather than hinder your natural delivery style. It's also important to be transparent with your congregation about the use of such technology, explaining how it serves to improve their experience of the message.

For those interested in the technical aspects of these artificial intelligence applications, our companion book, "AI for Novices," offers a deeper dive into the underlying technologies. However, for most pastors, a basic understanding of the capabilities and limitations of these tools is sufficient to harness their benefits effectively.

Artificial intelligence can also play a role in post-sermon analysis and improvement. Advanced systems can analyze recordings of your sermons, providing detailed feedback on various aspects of your delivery. They might identify patterns in your speech, moments where you tend to lose energy, or sections where your language becomes less clear. This kind of objective feedback can be invaluable for continuous improvement in your preaching ministry.

Pastor Michael, for instance, had always struggled with the feeling that his sermons weren't as impactful as they could be. After implementing an artificial intelligence analysis tool, he discovered that he tended to use complex theological terms without adequate explanation, potentially alienating less-versed members of his congregation. Armed with this insight, he was able to consciously adjust his language, resulting in more engaging and accessible sermons.

One intriguing possibility for the future of artificial intelligence in sermon delivery is the potential for adaptive sermons. While still in its early stages, this technology could allow for slight real-time adjustments to sermon content based on congregation response. For instance, if the system detects confusion during a particular point, it might prompt you to elaborate further or suggest a clarifying illustration.

However, as we consider such advanced applications, we must hold fast to the timeless truth articulated by Charles Spurgeon: "The power that is in the Gospel does not lie in the eloquence of the preacher, otherwise men would be the converters of souls, nor does it lie in the preacher's learning; otherwise it would consist in the wisdom of men. We might preach until our tongues rotted, till we would exhaust our lungs and die, but never a soul would be converted unless the Holy Spirit be with the Word of God to give it the power to convert the soul."

As we conclude our exploration of artificial intelligence in sermon delivery, it's clear that these tools offer exciting possibilities for enhancing our communication of God's truth. From real-time feedback to adaptive presentations, from accessibility enhancements to post-sermon analysis, artificial intelligence can serve as a valuable ally in our preaching ministry.

Yet, we must always remember that these are tools, not replacements for the essential elements of effective preaching: prayer, study, and reliance on the Holy Spirit. The goal of incorporating artificial intelligence into sermon delivery should be to remove barriers to communication, allowing the life-changing message of the Gospel to shine through more clearly.

As we move forward, embracing the possibilities of this new technology while staying rooted in timeless truths, we open ourselves to new ways of fulfilling our calling as ministers of God's Word. The fusion of ancient wisdom and cutting-edge technology offers an exciting frontier for preaching ministry, one that holds the potential to reach hearts and change lives in powerful new ways.

CHAPTER EIGHT

AI in Pastoral Care

Section 8.1: AI-Powered Counseling and Support Tools

The ministry of pastoral care stands at the heart of a shepherd's calling. It's in the quiet moments of counsel, the heartfelt prayers for the suffering, and the gentle guidance of the lost that the love of Christ shines brightest through His servants. In our rapidly evolving digital age, artificial intelligence offers intriguing possibilities to enhance and extend this vital aspect of ministry.

Imagine a world where the comforting presence of pastoral care is available at any hour, ready to offer a listening ear, scripturally-grounded advice, and a bridge to professional help when needed. This is the promise that artificial intelligence-powered counseling and support tools hold for the future of pastoral care.

Pastor Sarah leads a bustling suburban church, her days filled with sermon preparation, administrative tasks, and a steady stream of congregants seeking her counsel. Despite her best efforts, she often feels stretched thin, unable to provide the depth of care each person deserves. Recognizing this challenge, she decided to implement an artificial intelligence-powered counseling chatbot on her church's website.

The chatbot, grounded in biblical wisdom and trained on thousands of pastoral conversations, serves as a first point of contact for those seeking help. It offers a safe, anonymous space for individuals to express their concerns and receive immediate, scripturally-based guidance. For issues requiring human intervention, the system seamlessly connects users with Pastor Sarah or other qualified counselors.

One evening, a young man in the throes of a crisis of faith engaged with the chatbot. Through a series of thoughtful questions and responses, the artificial intelligence system helped him articulate his doubts and pointed him towards relevant scriptures and resources. By the end of the conversation, the young man felt heard and supported, scheduling an in-person meeting with Pastor Sarah to delve deeper into his questions.

However, as we embrace these technological aids, they should never replace the personal touch of pastoral care but rather extend its reach and effectiveness.

Another powerful application of artificial intelligence in pastoral counseling is in the realm of pattern recognition and early intervention. Advanced algorithms can analyze patterns in chatbot conversations, identifying recurring themes or potential red flags that might indicate a need for more intensive support.

For instance, Pastor Michael's church implemented an artificial intelligence system that monitored anonymous counseling chat logs. The system noticed a trend of increased discussions around financial stress and marital conflict. Armed with this insight, Pastor Michael was able to develop a targeted sermon series and support group addressing these specific challenges in his community.

Artificial intelligence can also play a crucial role in providing ongoing support between counseling sessions. Imagine a system that sends personalized daily devotionals, scripture readings, or encouraging messages based on an individual's specific struggles or goals. These digital touchpoints can help maintain momentum and provide continual reminders of God's love and truth.

Consider the story of Lisa, a member of Pastor David's congregation struggling with anxiety. After her initial counseling session, Lisa was connected with an artificial intelligence-powered support app. Each morning, she received a carefully selected scripture and brief meditation tailored to her situation. Throughout the day, the app would check in, offering breathing exercises, prayer prompts, or links to relevant resources. This consistent support helped Lisa apply the insights from her counseling sessions to her daily life, accelerating her journey towards healing.

However, in our enthusiasm for these new tools, we must be mindful of potential pitfalls. The use of artificial intelligence in pastoral care raises important ethical considerations around privacy, data security, and the limits of technology in addressing deeply personal and spiritual matters. As G.K. Chesterton wisely noted, "The Christian ideal has not been tried and found wanting. It has been found difficult; and left untried." We must ensure that our use of technology doesn't become a shortcut that bypasses the sometimes difficult but always essential personal engagement of pastoral care.

In practical terms, integrating artificial intelligence into pastoral care might involve a multi-layered approach. A chatbot or virtual assistant could serve as an initial point of contact, available 24/7 to offer immediate support and triage more serious issues. This could be complemented by an artificial intelligence-powered scheduling system that helps match individuals with the most appropriate counselor based on their needs and the counselor's expertise. Follow-up care could be enhanced through personalized devotional apps and check-in systems.

Artificial intelligence can also aid in the ongoing training and development of pastoral counselors. Advanced systems can simulate a wide range of counseling scenarios, allowing pastors and lay leaders to practice their skills in a safe, controlled environment. These simulations can provide immediate feedback, helping counselors refine their approach and identify areas for improvement.

Pastor Rachel, for example, used an artificial intelligence-powered training program to help prepare her team of lay counselors. The system presented them with complex scenarios involving issues like marital conflict, addiction, and spiritual doubt. As the counselors worked through these simulated sessions, the artificial intelligence provided real-time feedback on their responses, suggesting alternative approaches and highlighting potential blind spots. This training helped Rachel's team feel more confident and better prepared to handle real-life counseling situations.

One intriguing possibility for the future of artificial intelligence in pastoral care is the development of more sophisticated emotion recognition systems. These tools could potentially help pastors better understand and respond to the emotional state of those they're counseling, even in digital interactions. For instance, an artificial intelligence system might analyze voice patterns or written text to detect underlying emotions like anxiety, depression, or anger, alerting the pastor to issues that might not be explicitly stated.

However, as we consider such advanced applications, our use of artificial intelligence in pastoral care should always serve the higher purpose of helping individuals grow in their relationship with God and understand their identity in Christ.

As artificial intelligence continues to evolve, its potential applications in pastoral care are bound to expand. From more sophisticated counseling chatbots to virtual reality-based support groups, the possibilities are exciting. Yet, amidst this technological revolution, the heart of pastoral care remains unchanged: to reflect the love of Christ, to speak truth in love, and to guide people towards a deeper relationship with God.

In the next chapter, we'll explore how artificial intelligence can support another crucial aspect of pastoral care: crisis management. The ability to respond quickly and effectively in times of personal or community crisis is a vital part of a pastor's role, and artificial intelligence offers intriguing possibilities for enhancing this critical ministry.

Section 8.2: Chatbots for 24/7 Congregation Support

To further explore the potential of chatbots in congregational support, let's consider their role in fostering community connections. Many churches struggle with helping new members integrate into the life of the congregation. Artificial intelligence-powered chatbots can play a crucial role in this process.

Pastor Thomas implemented a welcome chatbot for his growing church. New visitors could interact with the chatbot to learn about various ministries, small groups, and upcoming events. The system would ask questions about their interests and family situation, then suggest relevant groups or activities. For instance, a young couple with children might be directed to the family ministry and introduced to upcoming parenting classes. This personalized approach helped newcomers feel welcomed and connected from their very first interaction with the church.

However, as churches embrace these technological solutions, they must be mindful of the potential for exclusion. Not all congregants may be comfortable with or have access to digital tools. Churches must ensure that their adoption of chatbot technology doesn't inadvertently create barriers for certain members of their community.

Another powerful application of chatbots in congregational support is in the area of prayer ministry. Many Christians struggle to maintain a consistent prayer life, often feeling unsure about how to pray or what to pray for. An artificial intelligence-powered prayer companion could provide valuable support in this area.

Imagine a chatbot that sends daily prayer prompts based on current events, the church calendar, or personal prayer requests submitted by the user. The system could guide users through different prayer models, such as the ACTS model (Adoration, Confession, Thanksgiving, Supplication) or the Lord's Prayer, providing scripture references and reflective questions along the way.

Pastor Maria implemented such a system in her church, calling it the "PrayerPartner" chatbot. Members could submit prayer requests through the chatbot, which would then distribute these requests to other users who had indicated a willingness to pray for others. The system would follow up with both the requester and the prayer partners, fostering a sense of connection and support within the congregation.

One user, Robert, found the PrayerPartner particularly helpful during a difficult period in his life. Struggling with unemployment, Robert submitted a prayer request through the chatbot. Over the next weeks, he received encouraging messages from the system, reminding him of God's faithfulness and letting him know that others in the congregation were praying for him. This consistent support helped Robert maintain hope and feel connected to his church family during a challenging time.

Yet, as churches implement these prayer support systems, they must be cautious not to reduce prayer to a merely mechanical exercise. As A.W. Tozer warned, "The danger is that we will merely learn to live with God rather than learning to live in Him." The goal of any prayer support tool should be to deepen the user's personal relationship with God, not to replace it with a digital substitute.

Chatbots can also play a valuable role in biblical education and discipleship. Many Christians desire to deepen their understanding of Scripture but struggle to find the time or resources to do so. An artificial intelligence-powered Bible study companion could help bridge this gap.

Pastor David's church developed a chatbot called "BibleBuddy" to support their congregation's spiritual growth. The system offered daily Bible readings, explanatory notes, and reflective questions. Users could ask the chatbot questions about the text, and it would provide answers based on reputable commentaries and theological resources. For more complex questions, the system would suggest relevant sermons from the church's archive or recommend books from the church library.

One church member, Lisa, found BibleBuddy particularly helpful as she read through the book of Romans. The chatbot's explanations of complex theological concepts and its ability to cross-reference related passages helped Lisa gain a deeper understanding of Paul's teachings. When she encountered a particularly challenging section, the chatbot suggested she attend an upcoming Bible study group focused on Romans, helping her connect with others wrestling with the same questions.

Chatbots can also serve as valuable tools for pastoral care in the area of habit formation and accountability. Many Christians struggle to develop and maintain spiritual disciplines such as regular Bible reading, prayer, or service. An artificial intelligence-powered accountability partner could provide gentle reminders and encouragement in these areas.

Pastor Sarah implemented a chatbot called "GrowthGuide" in her church. Members could set personal spiritual growth goals - such as reading the Bible for 15 minutes daily, praying for their neighbors once a week, or volunteering monthly at a local shelter. The chatbot would check in regularly, offering encouragement, tracking progress, and providing relevant resources.

For instance, James, a busy professional, set a goal to read through the New Testament in a year. GrowthGuide would send him daily reading reminders, ask reflective questions about the text, and offer encouragement when he fell behind. The system also connected James with a small group of others working towards similar goals, fostering a sense of community and mutual accountability.

As we look to the future, the potential applications of chatbots in congregational support seem boundless. We might see systems that can facilitate virtual small groups, connecting church members with similar interests or life stages for online fellowship and study. Or chatbots that can help coordinate complex service projects, matching volunteers with tasks based on their skills and availability.

However, as churches embrace these technological innovations, they must continually reflect on their impact on the nature of the Christian community and discipleship. How do we ensure that these digital tools enhance rather than replace face-to-face interactions? How do we maintain the personal touch of pastoral care in an increasingly digital ministry landscape?

These questions remind us that while artificial intelligence can be a powerful tool in pastoral care, it can never replace the fundamental elements of Christian ministry: the guidance of the Holy Spirit, the truth of God's Word, and the power of human compassion and connection. As we navigate this new frontier of digital ministry, may we always remember that our ultimate goal is not technological innovation but drawing people into a deeper relationship with the living God.

Section 8.3: The Role of AI in Crisis Management

The role of artificial intelligence in crisis management within pastoral care represents a frontier where cutting-edge technology meets age-old human needs. In times of personal or community crisis, the ability to respond swiftly, compassionately, and effectively can make a profound difference in people's lives and their faith journeys.

Pastor Rachel's vibrant urban church faced an unexpected challenge when a devastating hurricane struck their city. As floodwaters rose and power lines fell, her congregation was scattered, scared, and desperately needed support. In this moment of chaos, the church's artificial intelligence-powered crisis management system proved its worth.

The system, which Rachel had implemented months earlier, sprang into action. It began by sending automated wellness checks to every member of the congregation via text and email. Those who didn't respond within a certain timeframe were flagged for personal follow-up. Artificial intelligence analyzes the responses, categorizes needs, and prioritizes the most urgent cases for immediate attention.

One elderly couple, the Johnsons, reported being trapped in their home with rising water and dwindling supplies. The system immediately alerted Pastor Rachel and the crisis response team, providing the couple's location and specific needs. A rescue team was dispatched within hours, and the Johnsons were brought to safety.

This scenario illustrates the potential of artificial intelligence to enhance crisis response in pastoral care.

Artificial intelligence's capabilities in crisis management extend beyond mere communication and triage. Advanced systems can analyze patterns in crisis data, helping church leaders anticipate and prepare for potential issues before they escalate.

For instance, Pastor Michael's church, located in an area prone to wildfires, implemented an artificial intelligence system that monitored local weather patterns, fire department alerts, and social media activity. When conditions suggest an increased risk of wildfires, the system automatically initiates preparedness protocols, such as updating evacuation plans, checking on vulnerable members, and mobilizing volunteer teams.

During one arid summer, the system detected early signs of a potential wildfire threat. It alerted Pastor Michael, who was able to activate the church's emergency response plan days before an official evacuation order was issued. This proactive approach allowed the church to serve as a hub of support and information for the community, embodying Christ's love tangibly during a crisis.

One of the most potent aspects of artificial intelligence in crisis management is its ability to learn and improve over time. Machine learning algorithms allow these systems to analyze past crises, identifying what worked well and what could be improved. This continuous learning process allows for more effective responses to future emergencies.

Pastor Lisa's church, which serves a large college student population, found its artificial intelligence system particularly helpful during exam seasons when stress-related crises often peaked. The system learned to recognize patterns in the issues students faced and the support that proved most effective. Over time, it became adept at predicting potential crises and suggesting preventative measures, such as scheduling additional counseling hours or organizing stress-relief events during high-risk periods.

However, implementing artificial intelligence in crisis management is not without its challenges. Privacy concerns, the potential for overreliance on technology, and the risk of missing nuanced human needs are all factors that must be carefully considered.

In practical terms, implementing an artificial intelligence system for crisis management involves several key steps. First, church leaders must clearly define a crisis and establish protocols for different emergencies. Next, the system must be populated with a comprehensive database of resources, including emergency services, mental health professionals, and community aid organizations. Finally, there must be a plan for regular drills and system updates to ensure readiness for real crises.

Our companion book, AI for Novices, offers a more in-depth exploration of the technical aspects of crisis management systems.

One intriguing application of artificial intelligence in crisis management is post-crisis care and recovery. Imagine a system that can provide personalized support plans for individuals or families recovering from a crisis, offering tailored resources, scripture readings, and check-ins based on their specific situation and needs.

Pastor David implemented such a system in his church following layoffs at a significant local employer. The artificial intelligence-powered recovery support system offered affected families customized financial advice, job search resources, and spiritual encouragement. It also connected them with others in similar situations, fostering a support network within the church community.

One church member, Sarah, found this system particularly helpful after losing her job. The daily scriptures and encouragement messages helped her maintain hope, while the practical resources assisted in her job search. When Sarah secured a new position three months later, she credited the consistent support from her church, facilitated by the artificial intelligence system, as a critical factor in helping her through the crisis.

As we look to the future, the potential applications of artificial intelligence in crisis management seem boundless. We might see systems that can coordinate large-scale disaster response efforts across multiple churches and organizations or artificial intelligence-powered virtual reality simulations for crisis response training.

Implementing artificial intelligence in crisis management raises essential questions about the nature of pastoral care and the role of technology in ministry. How do we balance the efficiency and scale of artificial intelligence-powered responses with the need for personal, human touch in times of crisis? How can we ensure that our use of technology enhances, rather than diminishes, our capacity for empathy and compassion?

As we navigate this new frontier of digital ministry, may we always remember that our ultimate goal is to manage crises effectively and bring people into a more profound experience of God's love and care, even amid life's storms.

In exploring artificial intelligence in pastoral care, we've journeyed from counseling support to 24/7 chatbots and crisis management. Each application brings opportunities and challenges, reminding us of the complex interplay between technology and ministry. As we move forward, we must continue to seek wisdom in integrating these powerful tools into our pastoral practice, always focusing on the One, our ultimate source of help in times of trouble.

CHAPTER NINE

AI in Worship and Music Ministry

Section 9.1: AI-Generated Worship Music and Lyrics

In sanctuaries across the world, the melodies of praise have long been a cornerstone of Christian worship. From ancient Psalms to modern choruses, music serves as a powerful medium for expressing devotion and experiencing the divine. Now, as technology advances, artificial intelligence emerges as an unexpected collaborator in this sacred art form, offering new pathways for creative worship.

The landscape of worship music is evolving, with artificial intelligence systems now capable of composing melodies and crafting lyrics that resonate with timeless themes of faith. These systems, trained on vast libraries of existing worship songs, learn to mimic the structures, harmonies, and lyrical patterns that define effective worship music. The result is a blend of familiar comfort and fresh inspiration.

One platform making waves in this arena is Suno.com. Though not exclusively designed for worship music, Suno's artificial intelligence capabilities have caught the attention of forward-thinking worship leaders. The platform allows users to input themes or prompts, which the system then transforms into full-fledged songs, complete with vocals and instrumentation.

Pastor Sarah, who shepherds a diverse congregation in a bustling urban center, recently experimented with Suno.com. Preparing for a series on divine grace, she fed the platform with key concepts and scriptures. "The results were astounding," she recounts. "The artificial intelligence composed a song that captured the essence of unmerited favor in a way I hadn't considered. It was as if the machine had tapped into a wellspring of creativity, offering a fresh perspective on an age-old truth."

This anecdote illuminates a crucial point: artificial intelligence in worship music isn't about supplanting human creativity but enhancing and inspiring it. Tools like Suno.com provide a springboard for ideas, which worship leaders can then mold and refine to suit their congregation's unique spiritual needs.

However, the integration of artificial intelligence into this hallowed space raises important questions. Some argue that worship music, as a form of heartfelt prayer and praise, should originate solely from human experience and emotion. They wonder if a machine, regardless of its sophistication, can truly capture the depth of spiritual connection.

To navigate these concerns, we might turn to the wisdom of Christian thinkers who have contemplated the relationship between faith and human innovation. G.K. Chesterton, known for his keen insights on faith and culture, once wrote, "Art, like morality, consists of drawing the line somewhere." In the context of artificial intelligence-generated worship music, this line drawing becomes a thoughtful process of discernment, blending technological capabilities with spiritual authenticity.

Moreover, the use of artificial intelligence in creating worship music can be viewed as a continuation of the church's long-standing tradition of employing cutting-edge tools to glorify God. Just as the great composers of hymns embraced new musical instruments and styles in their time, today's worship leaders can harness artificial intelligence to craft songs of praise that resonate with contemporary congregations.

It's crucial to note that artificial intelligence systems like Suno.com don't operate in isolation. They require the guiding hand of spiritually grounded individuals who bring theological understanding and pastoral sensitivity to the process. This human touch ensures that the generated content aligns with biblical truths and meets the specific needs of the faith community.

For instance, Pastor Sarah's experience with Suno.com involved a process of collaborative refinement. While the artificial intelligence provided a unique melodic structure and lyrical framework, she worked with her worship team to adjust phrases, incorporate specific scriptural references, and ensure the song's theology aligned with their church's doctrinal positions.

The process of using artificial intelligence in worship music creation is not without its challenges. One significant hurdle is the need for discernment when selecting and refining the output. Not every artificially generated song will be suitable for worship, and it takes a keen spiritual ear to distinguish between what enhances worship and what might detract from it.

Consider the experience of Worship Director Mark at a suburban megachurch. He shares, "When we first started experimenting with artificial intelligence-generated music, we were overwhelmed by the sheer volume of content it produced. It took time to develop a process for sifting through the material and identifying the gems that truly spoke to our congregation's heart."

This experience highlights the importance of maintaining a strong theological foundation when incorporating artificial intelligence into worship music creation. It's not enough to simply accept whatever the system generates; rather, it requires a thoughtful, prayerful approach to selection and adaptation.

Another consideration is the potential impact on the role of human worship leaders and musicians. Some fear that artificial intelligence might diminish the need for these vital ministry roles. However, proponents argue that artificial intelligence should be seen as a tool to augment and inspire human creativity, not replace it.

John Stott, the renowned evangelical leader and writer, once said, "The Christian mind is the prerequisite of Christian thinking. And Christian thinking is the prerequisite of Christian action." Applying this wisdom to our context, we can see that the thoughtful, Spirit-led application of artificial intelligence in worship music is key to its effective use.

As we explore this new frontier, it's essential to consider the theological implications of using artificial intelligence in worship. Does the use of machine-generated content in any way diminish the authenticity of our worship? How do we ensure that the focus remains on glorifying God rather than marveling at technological capabilities?

To address these questions, we can look to Scripture for guidance. The Apostle Paul writes in 1 Corinthians 10:31, "So, whether you eat or drink, or whatever you do, do all to the glory of God." This verse reminds us that our use of technology, including artificial intelligence, should ultimately serve the purpose of honoring God.

297

As we continue to explore the potential of artificial intelligence in worship music, it's important to maintain a balance between embracing innovation and preserving the heart of worship. Artificial intelligence should be seen as a creative partner in the worship-making process, not a replacement for Spirit-led human contribution. The goal is to enhance, not diminish, the profound connection between worshippers and their Creator.

Looking ahead, the potential applications of artificial intelligence in worship music are vast. Imagine a system that could generate personalized worship songs based on a believer's prayer journal entries or an artificial intelligence assistant that helps worship leaders quickly arrange complex harmonies for their choir. These possibilities, while exciting, must always be approached with discernment and a commitment to authentic worship.

One intriguing possibility is the use of artificial intelligence to help churches develop culturally relevant worship music. In an increasingly diverse world, many congregations struggle to create music that resonates with multiple cultural backgrounds. Artificial intelligence could potentially analyze various cultural music styles and blend them with traditional hymns or contemporary worship songs, creating unique fusions that speak to multicultural congregations.

Pastor David, who leads a diverse inner-city church, shares his experience: "We used an artificial intelligence tool to help us create a song that blended gospel, hip-hop, and traditional hymn elements. The result was a powerful piece of music that united our congregation in worship, bridging generational and cultural gaps."

However, as we embrace these technological advancements, we must also be mindful of potential pitfalls. There's a risk of becoming overly reliant on artificial intelligence, potentially stifling the organic, Spirit-led creativity that has long been a hallmark of powerful worship music. We must strike a balance, using artificial intelligence as a tool to enhance our worship, not define it.

Additionally, there are important copyright and ethical considerations to address. As artificial intelligence systems learn from existing worship songs, questions arise about intellectual property rights and the originality of the generated content. Churches and worship leaders must navigate these waters carefully, ensuring they respect the rights of original composers while also fostering innovation.

Despite these challenges, the potential benefits of artificial intelligence in worship music are significant. It can serve as a powerful tool for inspiration, helping to break through creative blocks and offering fresh perspectives on timeless truths. It can also be a valuable resource for smaller churches or those in remote areas, providing access to high-quality musical resources that might otherwise be out of reach.

As we look to the future, it's clear that artificial intelligence will play an increasingly significant role in many aspects of ministry, including worship music. The key will be to approach this technology with wisdom, discernment, and a steadfast commitment to authentic, Spirit-led worship.

In the words of A.W. Tozer, "What comes into our minds when we think about God is the most important thing about us." As we incorporate artificial intelligence into our worship practices, we must ensure that it serves to elevate our thoughts of God, deepening our understanding of His character and drawing us closer to Him.

In the following sections, we'll explore how artificial intelligence is being used to tailor worship experiences and integrate with existing church technologies. We'll examine the practical applications of these tools and consider their potential impact on the future of music ministry. As we embark on this exploration, let us approach the topic with open minds and prayerful hearts, seeking to honor God in all our innovations.

The journey of integrating artificial intelligence into worship music is just beginning. It promises to be a path filled with exciting possibilities, challenges to overcome, and opportunities for growth. As we navigate this new terrain, may we always remember that our ultimate goal is not technological advancement for its own sake but the glorification of God and the edification of His people.

Section 9.2: Personalizing Worship Experiences with AI

As we delve deeper into the realm of artificial intelligence in worship, we encounter a fascinating frontier: the personalization of worship experiences. This concept, while revolutionary, builds upon a fundamental truth of Christian faith - that our relationship with God is deeply personal and unique.

Imagine entering your church's sanctuary on a Sunday morning. As you settle into your seat, the worship team begins to play. The melody seems familiar, yet subtly different. The lyrics resonate with you on a profound level, speaking directly to your current spiritual journey. This isn't a coincidence; it's the result of artificial intelligence working behind the scenes to tailor the worship experience to the congregation's collective needs and individual spiritual states.

The potential for artificial intelligence to personalize worship experiences is vast and multifaceted. At its core, this technology aims to create a more engaging, relevant, and meaningful worship environment for each individual. But how exactly does this work, and what are the implications for our churches?

One pioneering approach involves the use of data analytics coupled with artificial intelligence. Churches that have embraced digital giving or mobile apps often have access to a wealth of data about their congregants' engagement patterns. When this information is fed into an artificial intelligence system, it can identify trends and preferences that might not be immediately apparent to human observers.

Pastor James, who leads a tech-savvy megachurch in Silicon Valley, shares his experience: "We implemented an artificial intelligence system that analyzes data from our church app - things like which devotionals people read, what prayer requests they submit, even which songs they listen to most often. This information helps our worship team curate setlists that truly resonate with where our congregation is spiritually."

However, this approach raises important questions about privacy and the appropriate use of personal data in a church context. It's crucial for church leaders to be transparent about how they're using technology and to give congregants the option to opt out if they're uncomfortable.

Another exciting application of artificial intelligence in personalizing worship experiences is through adaptive lyric displays. Some churches are experimenting with systems that can subtly alter the lyrics projected on screens based on the congregation's demographics or current events affecting the community.

For example, in a church located in an area recently hit by natural disasters, artificial intelligence might suggest emphasizing lyrics about God's protection and comfort. In a congregation with many young families, it might highlight lyrics about God's love for children. These subtle shifts can help make familiar songs feel freshly relevant.

Worship leader Sarah from a mid-sized church in the Midwest explains, "Our adaptive lyric system has been a game-changer. It helps us strike a balance between the familiarity of beloved hymns and the need for contextual relevance. It's like having a collaborative partner that helps us fine-tune our worship in real-time."

The concept of personalized worship experiences extends beyond just music. Some churches are using artificial intelligence to create customized devotional content or prayer prompts based on individual members' spiritual growth patterns and expressed needs.

However, as we explore these possibilities, we must grapple with some profound theological questions. Does personalizing worship risk creating a consumer-driven church experience that caters to individual preferences rather than challenging believers to grow? How do we balance personalization with the communal aspect of worship?

To address these concerns, we can turn to the wisdom of Christian thinkers who have wrestled with the tension between individual and communal faith expressions. Dietrich Bonhoeffer, in his book "Life Together," emphasizes the importance of the Christian community while also acknowledging the unique journey of each believer. He writes, "The Christian needs another Christian who speaks God's Word to him. He needs him again and again when he becomes uncertain and discouraged."

In light of this, we can view artificial intelligence-driven personalization not as a replacement for communal worship but as a tool to enhance both individual and collective spiritual growth. The key is to use these technologies in a way that draws people deeper into the community rather than isolating them in personalized bubbles.

As we navigate this new territory, it's crucial to maintain a strong theological foundation. John Piper, in his book "Desiring God," reminds us that the ultimate goal of worship is not our personal satisfaction but God's glory. He writes, "God is most

glorified in us when we are most satisfied in Him."
With this perspective, we can see personalized
worship experiences as a means to help individuals
connect more deeply with God, thereby bringing Him
greater glory.

Looking ahead, the potential for artificial intelligence
to personalize worship experiences is both exciting
and challenging. Future developments might include
AI-powered prayer assistants that help individuals
articulate their deepest spiritual longings or virtual
reality worship experiences that adapt to each user's
spiritual state.

However, as we embrace these innovations, we must
remain vigilant. The goal should always be to use
technology as a tool for deepening faith and fostering
genuine community, not as a shortcut to spiritual
growth or a substitute for human-to-human
connection.

In the words of C.S. Lewis, "The Church exists for
nothing else but to draw men into Christ, to make

them little Christ." As we explore the use of artificial intelligence in personalizing worship, may we never lose sight of this fundamental purpose. Let us use these tools wisely and prayerfully, always seeking to draw people closer to Christ and to one another.

As we move forward, we'll examine how artificial intelligence is being integrated into existing worship technology, creating new possibilities for engaging and meaningful worship experiences. We'll explore the practical applications of these tools and consider their potential impact on the future of worship ministry. Through it all, may we approach this journey with open minds, discerning hearts, and an unwavering commitment to honoring God in all we do.

Section 9.3: Integrating AI into Worship Technology

The sanctuary hums with anticipation as the congregation settles in for the Sunday service. Unbeknownst to many, an invisible intelligence works alongside the worship team, seamlessly blending technology and spirituality. This is the new frontier of worship technology, where artificial intelligence enhances every aspect of the experience.

At Crossroads Community Church, Pastor Lisa watches as her tech team makes final adjustments to their AI-powered worship system. "It's remarkable," she muses, "how far we've come from the days of overhead projectors and cassette tapes."

The church's new intelligent lighting system springs to life, bathing the sanctuary in a warm glow that subtly shifts with the mood of each song. No lighting technician frantically adjusts controls; the AI analyzes the music in real time, creating a visual atmosphere that complements the worship.

As the first chords of "Amazing Grace" fill the air, the sound system kicks into gear. Gone are the days of screeching feedback and muddy mixes. The AI-driven audio processor continuously monitors and adjusts the sound, ensuring crystal-clear quality from the front row to the balcony.

"Our sound volunteers used to spend hours tweaking settings," Pastor Lisa explains. "Now, they're free to actually participate in worship. The system handles the technical details, allowing our team to focus on the spiritual aspects of the service."

On the massive screens flanking the stage, lyrics appear with perfect timing. The AI anticipates each line, eliminating the awkward pauses that once plagued less tech-savvy volunteers. But this system goes beyond simple lyric display. It analyzes the congregation's engagement through subtle cues - singing volume, body language, even facial expressions - and provides real-time feedback to the worship leader's in-ear monitors.

Jake, the worship pastor, finds this feature invaluable. "It's like having a direct line to the congregation's heart," he says. "I can sense when a particular song is really resonating and when it might be time to transition. It's helped us create more meaningful, Spirit-led worship experiences."

However, the integration of AI into worship technology extends far beyond audiovisuals. At Crossroads, they've implemented an intelligent prayer request system. Congregants can submit requests via a mobile app, which the AI analyzes for common themes and urgent needs. This information is then relayed to the pastoral team, helping them address the most pressing concerns of their flock in real time.

"It's transformed how we minister to our congregation," Pastor Lisa notes. "We're able to be more responsive and targeted in our prayers and support. It's like having a finger on the pulse of our church family at all times."

The system even extends to the sermon itself. As Pastor Lisa preaches, an AI-powered fact-checker runs in the background, verifying scriptural references and historical facts. If she misspeaks or needs additional information, a gentle prompt appears on her tablet, allowing for seamless correction or elaboration.

However, this level of technological integration isn't without its challenges. Some members of Crossroads' congregation have expressed concern about the perceived loss of the human touch in worship. "We've had to be intentional about balancing technology with authentic, personal interaction," Pastor Lisa admits. "We never want the AI to replace genuine human connection and Spirit-led worship."

To address these concerns, Crossroads has implemented "unplugged" services once a month, where they strip back the technology and focus on acoustic worship and personal testimonies. "It's about finding the right balance," Jake explains. "We use the AI to enhance our worship, not to replace the human element."

The church has also had to grapple with ethical considerations surrounding data privacy and the use of AI in sacred spaces. They've implemented strict data protection policies and are transparent with the congregation about how the technology is used.

This transparency is crucial, as it addresses one of the primary concerns about AI integration in worship - the fear of manipulation or loss of authenticity. By openly discussing how the technology is used and its limitations, Crossroads has been able to maintain trust with its congregation while embracing innovation.

The journey to this point wasn't without its bumps. Pastor Lisa recalls the initial skepticism from some church elders when the idea of AI integration was first proposed. "There was a fear that we were trying to automate worship, to remove the human and divine elements from our services," she says. "It took a lot of conversation and demonstration to show that our goal was exactly the opposite - to use technology to create space for deeper, more meaningful worship experiences."

One of the most powerful arguments in favor of the AI system came from an unexpected source - the church's ministry to the deaf and hard of hearing. The AI's ability to provide real-time, highly accurate closed captioning has made services more accessible than ever before. Sarah, a deaf member of the congregation, shares, "For the first time, I feel fully part of the worship experience. I'm not just seeing someone interpret; I'm getting the full context, the emotion, and even the musical notes described. It's opened up a whole new dimension of worship for me."

This accessibility extends to other areas as well. The church's AI system includes a translation module, providing real-time subtitles in multiple languages. In a diverse community like Crossroads, this feature has been transformative. "We've seen our international ministry grow exponentially," Pastor Lisa notes. "People who were hesitant to attend because of language barriers now feel welcomed and included."

The impact of AI on the music ministry has been particularly profound. In addition to the real-time mixing and lighting adjustments, the system has become a valuable tool for composition and arrangement. Jake explains, "We can input a theme or a Bible verse, and the AI will generate musical motifs or even full song structures. It's not about replacing human creativity but about inspiring and augmenting it. Some of our most powerful worship songs have come from this human-AI collaboration."

This collaborative approach extends to other areas of ministry as well. The church's small group ministry now uses AI-powered discussion guides that adapt based on the group's responses and engagement levels. "It's like having a skilled facilitator in every group," says Mark, the small group coordinator. "The AI can sense when a topic is resonating and suggest deeper questions, or recognize when the conversation is stalling and offer a new direction."

As with any technological advancement, there have been unexpected challenges and surprising benefits. One challenge came in the form of "AI dependency" among some of the ministry teams. "We had to remind everyone that the AI is a tool, not a replacement for spiritual discernment," Pastor Lisa explains. "We've had to be intentional about cultivating spiritual disciplines and maintaining a strong prayer life alongside our use of technology."

On the flip side, one unexpected benefit has been the AI's ability to identify patterns and trends in the spiritual life of the congregation. By analyzing sermon responses, prayer requests, and small group discussions, the system can provide insights into the collective spiritual journey of the church. "It's helped us tailor our teaching and ministry efforts to meet people where they are," Pastor Lisa says. "We can see when there's a widespread struggle with a particular issue or when there's a hunger for deeper teaching on a specific topic."

Looking to the future, Pastor Lisa sees even more potential for AI in worship technology. She envisions personalized devotional content delivered to congregants based on their spiritual growth patterns, AI-assisted pastoral counseling tools, and even virtual reality prayer rooms that adapt to individual needs.

"The possibilities are exciting," she says, "but we always come back to our core mission - bringing people closer to God. If the technology serves that purpose, we embrace it. If it becomes a distraction, we reevaluate."

This constant reevaluation is key to Crossroads' approach. They've established an AI ethics committee comprised of tech experts, theologians, and lay members, to regularly review their use of technology and its impact on the church's mission and values.

As the service at Crossroads draws to a close, the AI system fades the lights and music, creating a peaceful atmosphere for reflection. The congregation files out, many unaware of the invisible intelligence that helped shape their worship experience. And perhaps that's the mark of truly integrated worship technology - when it enhances the experience so seamlessly that it becomes invisible, allowing the focus to remain where it belongs - on God.

Yet, as they leave, some congregants linger, discussing the service. "Did you notice how the lighting seemed to match the mood of each song perfectly?" one asks. "And the way the pastor had that extra bit of information about Paul's journey right when someone asked about it—that was amazing!"

These conversations highlight an important truth - while the goal is for the technology to be seamless, its impact is still felt and appreciated. It's not about creating a flashy, tech-driven spectacle but about using every tool available to create an environment conducive to genuine worship and spiritual growth.

As Pastor Lisa locks up the church, she reflects on the journey they've taken. "Five years ago, I never would have imagined our church would be at the forefront of AI integration in worship," she muses. "But here we are, not just using this technology, but helping to shape its development in a way that honors God and serves His people."

She pauses at the door, looking back at the now-quiet sanctuary. "In the end, it's not about the technology. It's about the lives that have changed, the hearts touched, and the spirits lifted. If AI can help us do that more effectively, then I believe we're using it exactly as God intended - as a tool to bring His children closer to Him."

With that thought, she steps out into the sunlight, ready to face whatever new challenges and opportunities the intersection of faith and technology might bring in the weeks and months to come.

CHAPTER TEN

AI in Church Administration

Section 10.1: Streamlining Church Operations with AI

The integration of artificial intelligence into church administration marks a significant shift in how religious organizations manage their day-to-day operations. This technology offers churches the ability to streamline processes, analyze data more effectively, and ultimately free up human resources for more spiritually focused-tasks.

One of the primary areas where artificial intelligence proves invaluable is in membership management. Traditional methods of tracking attendance, managing contact information, and monitoring member engagement often involve time-consuming, manual processes. Artificial intelligence systems can automate these tasks, providing real-time updates and insights.

For example, Cornerstone Baptist Church implemented an artificial intelligence-powered membership system that automatically logs attendance through facial recognition technology. This not only saves time but also provides accurate data for trend analysis. The system can identify patterns in attendance, alerting church leaders to members who may have become disengaged and potentially need pastoral care.

Financial management is another area where artificial intelligence shines in church administration. Many churches struggle with budgeting, expense tracking, and financial forecasting. Artificial intelligence systems can analyze spending patterns, predict future financial needs, and even suggest areas where costs could be reduced.

Pastor Robert of Grace Community Church shares, "Our artificial intelligence financial system has been a game-changer. It identified that we were overspending on utilities and suggested energy-saving measures that have saved us thousands of dollars annually. That's money we can now put towards our community outreach programs."

Event planning and facility management also benefit from artificial intelligence integration. These systems can optimize room usage based on group sizes and equipment needs, schedule maintenance tasks, and even predict when equipment might need replacement based on usage patterns.

However, the implementation of artificial intelligence in church administration is not without challenges. There's often a learning curve for staff members who are used to traditional methods. Additionally, there can be concerns about data privacy and the depersonalization of church operations.

To address these issues, it's crucial for church leaders to approach artificial intelligence implementation with clear communication and proper training. As John Stott once said, "Knowledge is indispensable to Christian life and service. If we do not use the mind that God has given us, we condemn ourselves to spiritual superficiality." This wisdom applies equally to embracing new technologies that can enhance our ministry.

It's also important to remember that artificial intelligence should supplement, not replace, human interaction in church administration. The goal is to use this technology to handle routine tasks more efficiently, freeing up staff and volunteers to focus on relationship-building and spiritual care.

Looking ahead, the potential for artificial intelligence in church administration continues to grow. Predictive analytics could help churches anticipate community needs and plan outreach efforts more effectively. Natural language processing could assist in analyzing sermon feedback and helping pastors tailor their messages to their congregation's spiritual needs.

As churches continue to explore the possibilities of artificial intelligence in administration, it's crucial to approach this technology with discernment and intentionality. When implemented thoughtfully, artificial intelligence can be a powerful tool for enhancing ministry effectiveness and allowing church leaders to focus more fully on their spiritual calling.

For those interested in the technical aspects of implementing artificial intelligence in church administration, our companion book, "AI for Novices," provides in-depth guidance on choosing and setting up these systems. However, the focus here is on the practical applications and benefits of ministry.

As we move forward, we'll explore how artificial intelligence can enhance financial management and stewardship in churches, providing tools for more effective resource allocation and transparent financial reporting.

Section 10.2: AI for Financial Management and Stewardship

As we delve deeper into the application of artificial intelligence in church financial management, it's crucial to explore the specific tools and techniques that are transforming this aspect of ministry. One such tool is machine learning, a subset of artificial intelligence that enables systems to learn and improve from experience without being explicitly programmed. In the context of church finances, machine learning algorithms can analyze spending patterns, identify potential areas of waste, and even detect fraudulent activities.

For example, Harvest Community Church implemented a machine learning system to review its procurement processes. The system quickly identified that the church was ordering office supplies from multiple vendors at varying prices. By consolidating orders and negotiating bulk discounts, the church was able to reduce its office supply expenses by 15% annually. This seemingly small change, made possible by artificial intelligence, freed up resources that could be redirected toward ministry initiatives.

Another powerful application of artificial intelligence in financial stewardship is donor management and relationship building. Artificial intelligence-powered Customer Relationship Management (CRM) systems can analyze giving patterns, engagement levels, and communication preferences of individual donors. This granular level of insight allows churches to tailor their stewardship approaches, ensuring that each member of the congregation feels valued and understood.

Consider the experience of Lighthouse Fellowship, a growing church that struggled with donor retention. By implementing an artificial intelligence-driven CRM system, they were able to segment their donor base and create personalized communication strategies for each group. For instance, first-time givers received a series of welcome emails and invitations to newcomer events, while long-term supporters were kept informed about the impact of their contributions through targeted impact reports. As a result,

Lighthouse Fellowship saw a 30% increase in recurring donations and a significant improvement in overall donor satisfaction.

Artificial intelligence also plays a crucial role in grant management, an often overlooked aspect of church finance. Many churches rely on grants from foundations or government agencies to fund specific programs or initiatives. The grant application process can be complex and time-consuming, but artificial intelligence can streamline this process. Natural Language Processing (NLP) algorithms can analyze grant requirements, match them with church programs, and even assist in drafting compelling grant proposals.

First Presbyterian Church, for instance, used an artificial intelligence-powered grant management system to identify suitable grant opportunities for their youth outreach program. The system not only found relevant grants but also provided insights on successful application strategies based on historical data. As a result, the church secured a major grant that allowed them to expand their youth ministry significantly.

While the benefits of artificial intelligence in financial management are clear, it's important to address potential concerns and challenges. One common apprehension is the fear that artificial intelligence might replace human jobs in church administration. However, the reality is that artificial intelligence is not meant to replace humans but to augment their capabilities. By automating routine tasks, artificial intelligence frees up staff to focus on more strategic, relationship-oriented aspects of financial stewardship.

As G.K. Chesterton once said, "The real trouble with this world of ours is not that it is an unreasonable world, nor even that it is a reasonable one. The commonest kind of trouble is that it is nearly reasonable but not quite." This insight applies well to the implementation of artificial intelligence in church finances. While artificial intelligence can provide immense benefits, it's crucial to maintain a balance and not rely on it blindly.

For instance, while artificial intelligence can provide valuable insights into giving patterns and financial trends, the final decisions on budget allocations and stewardship strategies should always involve human discernment and prayer. The role of church leaders is to interpret the data provided by artificial intelligence through the lens of their spiritual calling and the specific needs of their congregation.

Privacy and data security are other important considerations when implementing artificial intelligence in church financial systems. Churches handle the sensitive financial information of their members, and it's crucial to ensure that this data is protected. When choosing artificial intelligence-powered financial management systems, churches should prioritize vendors that adhere to strict data protection standards and provide robust security measures.

Moreover, it's essential to maintain transparency about the use of artificial intelligence in financial management. Congregations should be informed about how their data is being used and the measures in place to protect their privacy. This transparency not only builds trust but also aligns with the biblical principle of integrity in all dealings.

The implementation of artificial intelligence in church financial management also opens up new possibilities for collaborative ministry. Cloud-based artificial intelligence systems allow for real-time financial reporting and collaborative decision-making, even when church leaders are geographically dispersed. This can be particularly beneficial for multi-site churches or denominations managing finances across multiple congregations.

For example, the Methodist Conference of Northern California implemented a cloud-based artificial intelligence financial management system across its 50 member churches. This allowed for centralized oversight of finances while still maintaining local autonomy. The system provided real-time financial dashboards for each church, as well as aggregated data for the conference leadership. This level of transparency and collaboration led to more efficient resource allocation and sharing of best practices across the conference.

As we look to the future, the potential of artificial intelligence in church financial management continues to expand. Emerging technologies like blockchain could revolutionize how churches handle transactions and maintain financial records. Blockchain's inherent transparency and immutability could provide an unprecedented level of accountability in church finances.

Additionally, advancements in natural language processing could make financial reports more accessible to the average church member. Imagine a system that could automatically generate easy-to-understand financial summaries, complete with visualizations, from complex accounting data. This could greatly enhance financial literacy within the congregation and encourage greater participation in financial stewardship.

However, as we embrace these technological advancements, it's crucial to remember the words of A.W. Tozer: "The Bible recognizes no faith that does not lead to obedience, nor does it recognize any obedience that does not spring from faith. The two are on opposite sides of the same coin." In the context of church financial management, this reminds us that while artificial intelligence can provide powerful tools, true stewardship springs from a heart of faith and obedience to God's calling.

Artificial intelligence in financial management and stewardship is not just about efficiency and accuracy; it's about multiplying the impact of every dollar entrusted to the church. By freeing up resources and providing deeper insights, artificial intelligence enables churches to be more effective in their mission of spreading the Gospel and serving their communities.

As we conclude this exploration of artificial intelligence in church financial management and stewardship, it's clear that these technologies offer immense potential for enhancing the administrative aspects of ministry. However, the true measure of success lies not in the sophistication of our tools but in how faithfully we use them to further God's kingdom.

In the next section, we'll shift our focus to another critical aspect of church administration: communication and outreach. We'll discover how artificial intelligence is breaking down barriers and creating new opportunities for churches to connect with their congregations and communities in meaningful ways.

Section 10.3: Enhancing Communication and Outreach

In the digital age, effective communication and outreach are paramount for churches seeking to fulfill their mission and engage with both their congregation and the wider community. Artificial intelligence has emerged as a powerful tool in this realm, offering innovative ways to connect, inform, and inspire. As we explore the intersection of artificial intelligence and church communication, we'll uncover how this technology is revolutionizing outreach efforts and fostering deeper connections within faith communities.

The landscape of communication has undergone a seismic shift in recent years, with digital platforms becoming increasingly central to how people interact and consume information. Churches, as pillars of community and bearers of timeless truths, must adapt to these changes while remaining true to their core message. Artificial intelligence provides a bridge between traditional ministry approaches and the digital world, offering tools that can amplify the church's voice and extend its reach.

One of the most impactful applications of artificial intelligence in church communication is in personalized content delivery. By analyzing data on individual members' interests, engagement patterns, and spiritual journeys, artificial intelligence systems can tailor communications to meet people where they are. This level of personalization ensures that each member receives content that is relevant, timely, and meaningful to their specific needs and circumstances.

Consider the experience of Cornerstone Community Church, which implemented an artificial intelligence-driven communication platform. The system analyzed members' interactions with previous church communications, their attendance at various events, and their volunteer activities. Based on this data, it created personalized weekly newsletters for each member, featuring content tailored to their interests and spiritual growth stage. As a result, the church saw a significant increase in email open rates and event attendance as members felt more connected and engaged with the church's activities.

Artificial intelligence also excels in optimizing the timing and frequency of communications. Through machine learning algorithms, these systems can determine the best times to send emails, post on social media, or push notifications to mobile apps for maximum engagement. This ensures that important messages don't get lost in the noise of our information-saturated world.

For instance, Grace Fellowship used an artificial intelligence tool to analyze their social media engagement patterns. The system identified that their congregation was most active on social platforms on Sunday afternoons and Wednesday evenings. By adjusting their posting schedule to align with these peak times, the church saw a 40% increase in engagement with their social media content, leading to greater awareness of church events and initiatives.

Natural Language Processing (NLP), another branch of artificial intelligence, is transforming how churches interact with their communities online. Chatbots powered by NLP can provide instant responses to common queries, offer spiritual support, and even guide visitors through the process of connecting with the church. These tools ensure that someone is always available to engage with individuals seeking information or support, regardless of the time of day.

Harvest Church implemented an NLP-powered chatbot on its website to assist with visitor inquiries. The bot could answer questions about service times, provide directions to the church, and even offer a simple daily devotional. For more complex queries, the bot seamlessly transferred the conversation to a human staff member. This system not only improved the church's responsiveness but also freed up staff time to focus on more complex pastoral care needs.

Artificial intelligence is also enhancing the church's ability to gather and analyze feedback from the congregation. Sentiment analysis tools can process comments from social media, surveys, and other feedback channels to gauge the overall mood and concerns of the church community. This invaluable insight allows church leaders to address issues proactively and tailor their messaging to meet the congregation's needs.

When Lighthouse Baptist Church used a sentiment analysis tool to review feedback from their recent sermon series, they discovered that many members struggled with applying the teachings to their daily lives. Armed with this insight, the pastoral team developed a series of practical workshops and small group materials to complement the sermons, leading to greater engagement and spiritual growth within the congregation.

In outreach, artificial intelligence is opening new avenues for churches to connect with their local communities. Geotargeting and predictive analytics allow churches to identify areas of their community with the greatest needs and tailor their outreach efforts accordingly. This data-driven approach ensures that limited resources are used effectively to make the most significant impact.

For example, First Presbyterian Church used artificial intelligence to analyze demographic data and social indicators in their city. The system identified a neighborhood with a high concentration of single-parent families facing economic challenges. In response, the church launched a targeted outreach program offering after-school care, job skills training, and support groups. This focused approach allowed the church to impact an area of genuine need significantly.

As we embrace these technological advancements, it's crucial to remember the words of C.S. Lewis: "God whispers to us in our pleasures, speaks in our conscience, but shouts in our pains: it is His megaphone to rouse a deaf world." Artificial intelligence in church communication should not be seen as a replacement for the human touch but as a tool to amplify the church's voice and extend its reach in a noisy world.

However, implementing artificial intelligence in church communication is not without challenges. There's a delicate balance between leveraging data for personalization and respecting individual privacy. Churches must be transparent about their data usage practices and comply with relevant privacy regulations.

Moreover, there's a risk of over-relying on artificial intelligence and losing the ministry's personal, relational aspect. As John Stott wisely noted, "The Gospel is not a philosophy of life... it is the proclamation of what God has done in and through Christ." While artificial intelligence can enhance our communication strategies, the heart of the church's message must always be the Gospel's transformative power, delivered with genuine care and human connection.

Looking to the future, emerging technologies like augmented reality (AR) and virtual reality (VR) present exciting possibilities for church communication and outreach. Imagine virtual prayer rooms where people worldwide can gather to pray together or AR-enhanced Bible study apps that bring Scripture to life in new ways. Artificial intelligence will make these technologies more intuitive, personalized, and impactful as they mature.

In conclusion, artificial intelligence is revolutionizing how churches communicate and reach out to their congregations and communities. From personalized content delivery to data-driven outreach strategies, these tools enable churches to be more effective and responsive in their ministry efforts. However, as we harness these powerful technologies, we must never forget that they are a means to an end – tools to help us fulfill our divine calling to share God's love and truth with the world.

As we conclude our exploration of artificial intelligence in church administration, we've seen how these technologies can transform financial management, streamline operations, and enhance communication. In the next chapter, we'll turn our attention to the exciting realm of artificial intelligence in evangelism and outreach, discovering how these tools can help spread the Gospel message in innovative and impactful ways.

CHAPTER ELEVEN

AI in Evangelism and Outreach

Section 11.1: Reaching the Unreached with AI

In the grand tapestry of Christian ministry, evangelism and outreach stand as vibrant threads, weaving through the fabric of our faith and connecting us to the world beyond our church walls. As we venture into the 21st century, artificial intelligence emerges as a powerful tool capable of amplifying our efforts to reach the unreached and spread the life-changing message of the Gospel.

The Great Commission, given by Jesus Christ himself, calls us to "go and make disciples of all nations" (Matthew 28:19). This divine mandate has driven missionaries and evangelists for centuries, inspiring them to cross oceans, traverse deserts, and brave untold dangers to share the Good News. Today, artificial intelligence offers us new pathways to fulfill this ancient calling, breaking down barriers of language, culture, and geography that once seemed insurmountable.

Consider the story of New Life Community Church, a small congregation nestled in the heart of rural America. Despite their limited resources and remote location, they harbored a burning desire to impact the world for Christ. Through the implementation of artificial intelligence-driven translation tools, they were able to create a multilingual online ministry that reached far beyond their small town. Their weekly sermons, once heard by a few hundred locals, now touch thousands of lives across the globe, translated in real-time into dozens of languages.

This miraculous feat of communication reminds us of the day of Pentecost, when the disciples, filled with the Holy Spirit, spoke in tongues and were understood by people from every nation. While artificial intelligence may not be a divine miracle, it certainly serves as a modern-day tool to break down the barriers of Babel and unite the global church in understanding.

But the power of artificial intelligence in evangelism extends far beyond mere translation. Predictive analytics, a branch of artificial intelligence, allows churches to identify areas and demographics most receptive to the Gospel message. By analyzing vast amounts of data on social trends, cultural shifts, and community needs, artificial intelligence can guide outreach efforts with unprecedented precision.

Lighthouse Baptist Church embraced this approach in its urban ministry. Using artificial intelligence algorithms, they analyzed social media activity, community forums, and local news to identify neighborhoods grappling with issues of loneliness and social isolation. Armed with this insight, they launched targeted outreach programs, offering community gatherings, support groups, and opportunities for meaningful connections. The result? A significant increase in newcomers to their church, many of whom found not just a welcoming community but also a saving faith in Christ.

This data-driven approach to evangelism might seem cold or impersonal at first glance. However, when viewed through the lens of the parable of the lost sheep, we see it in a different light. Just as the shepherd left the ninety-nine to seek out the one lost sheep, artificial intelligence allows us to identify and reach out to those most in need of the Gospel message.

Artificial intelligence also shines in its ability to personalize evangelistic content. By analyzing an individual's online behavior, interests, and spiritual journey, artificial intelligence can tailor messages and resources to speak directly to their unique needs and questions. This level of personalization echoes the approach of the Apostle Paul, who famously became "all things to all people so that by all possible means I might save some" (1 Corinthians 9:22).

Grace Fellowship Church implemented this strategy through an artificial intelligence-powered chatbot on its website. The bot, trained on a vast database of apologetics resources and Scripture, could engage visitors in meaningful conversations about faith, answering questions and addressing doubts with sensitivity and biblical accuracy. For many seekers, this 24/7 availability of spiritual guidance became a crucial first step on their journey to faith.

However, as we embrace these technological marvels, we must heed the wisdom of John Stott, who reminds us that "the Gospel is not a philosophy of life... it is the proclamation of what God has done in and through Christ." Artificial intelligence should never replace the human touch in evangelism but rather enhance and extend our ability to share the unchanging truth of God's love.

The use of artificial intelligence in evangelism also raises important ethical considerations. As stewards of people's spiritual journeys, we must be vigilant about data privacy and respect for individual autonomy. The line between personalized outreach and invasion of privacy can be thin, and churches must navigate this landscape with wisdom and integrity.

Moreover, there's a risk of over-relying on artificial intelligence and losing sight of the supernatural element of evangelism. As A.W. Tozer wisely noted, "The Holy Spirit is the Spirit of life, and only He can raise the spiritually dead." While artificial intelligence can open doors and create opportunities, true conversion and spiritual rebirth remain the work of God alone.

Looking to the future, emerging technologies like virtual and augmented reality present exciting possibilities for evangelism and outreach. Imagine virtual reality experiences that allow people to "walk" through biblical narratives or augmented reality apps that overlay Christian perspectives on real-world situations. As these technologies mature, artificial intelligence will play a crucial role in making them more immersive, personalized, and impactful.

The integration of artificial intelligence into evangelism and outreach efforts represents a new frontier in fulfilling the Great Commission. It allows us to reach further, connect deeper, and share the Gospel more effectively than ever before. However, as

350

we harness these powerful tools, we must always remember the words of the prophet Zechariah: "Not by might, nor by power, but by my Spirit, says the Lord of hosts" (Zechariah 4:6).

In our next section, we'll explore how artificial intelligence is revolutionizing social media evangelism, opening new avenues for digital ministry and online community building. The digital realm presents both challenges and opportunities for sharing the Gospel, and artificial intelligence stands ready to help us navigate this complex landscape with wisdom and grace.

Section 11.2: AI for Social Media Evangelism

The digital landscape has become the new Roman road of our era, connecting billions of people across vast distances and diverse cultures. Social media platforms, in particular, have emerged as bustling marketplaces of ideas where the Gospel can be shared with unprecedented reach and immediacy. Artificial intelligence stands as a powerful ally in this digital mission field, offering tools and insights that can amplify our message and connect us with seekers in meaningful ways.

Imagine the Apostle Paul, with his zeal for spreading the Good News, having access to the global audience that social media provides. He would undoubtedly seize this opportunity with both hands, adapting his approach to reach people where they are. Today, artificial intelligence allows us to do just that, helping us navigate the complexities of social media evangelism with greater effectiveness and precision.

Hope Community Church embraced this digital frontier with open arms. They implemented an artificial intelligence-driven content strategy for their social media outreach. The system analyzed trending topics, popular hashtags, and user engagement patterns to suggest timely and relevant content ideas. By aligning biblical truths with current events and cultural conversations, the church saw a significant increase in its social media engagement, reaching far beyond its local community.

This approach echoes the wisdom of G.K. Chesterton, who once said, "The Christian ideal has not been tried and found wanting. It has been found difficult and left untried." Artificial intelligence helps us present the timeless truths of Christianity in ways that resonate with modern audiences, making the 'difficult' more accessible and engaging.

One of the most powerful applications of artificial intelligence in social media evangelism is audience segmentation and targeting. By analyzing user data and behavior patterns, artificial intelligence can help churches identify specific groups of people who may be more receptive to the Gospel message. This allows for more focused and effective outreach efforts.

Crossroads Baptist Church utilized this capability to great effect in its college ministry. The artificial intelligence system identified clusters of college students expressing feelings of loneliness, existential questions, or spiritual curiosity on social media. The church then crafted targeted content addressing these specific needs and concerns, resulting in a significant increase in engagement from college-aged individuals and several new attendees at their young adult events.

This targeted approach might raise eyebrows among those who view evangelism as a broad, indiscriminate proclamation. However, it aligns well with the biblical principle of becoming "all things to all people" (1 Corinthians 9:22). Just as Jesus tailored his parables to his audience, using familiar cultural references and addressing specific concerns, artificial intelligence allows us to customize our message for different segments of the digital population.

Artificial intelligence also excels in optimizing the timing and frequency of social media posts. Through machine learning algorithms, these systems can determine the best times to share content for maximum visibility and engagement. This ensures that our message doesn't get lost in the constant stream of information flooding social media feeds.

Grace Fellowship implemented an artificial intelligence-powered social media management tool that analyzed their followers' online behavior patterns. The system identified that their audience was most active and receptive during weekday lunch hours and Sunday evenings. By adjusting their posting schedule accordingly, the church saw a 50% increase in post engagement and a significant growth in their online community.

Natural Language Processing (NLP), another branch of artificial intelligence, is transforming how churches interact with their social media audience. NLP-powered chatbots can engage in meaningful conversations with users, answer questions about faith, and even provide spiritual support. These tools ensure that someone is always available to engage with seekers, regardless of the time of day.

New Life Church deployed an NLP chatbot on their Facebook page to assist with visitor inquiries. The bot could answer questions about church beliefs, service times, and even offer a simple daily devotional. For more complex spiritual questions, the bot seamlessly transferred the conversation to a trained volunteer. This system not only improved the church's responsiveness but also created new opportunities for personal connections and discipleship.

While artificial intelligence can help us optimize our digital presence, the heart of our message must always be the transformative power of God's love, especially in times of struggle and pain.

The use of artificial intelligence in social media evangelism also presents unique challenges and ethical considerations. There's a fine line between personalized outreach and invasive targeting. Churches must be transparent about their data usage and respect individual privacy, always prioritizing ethical considerations over mere effectiveness.

Moreover, there's a risk of social media evangelism becoming impersonal or manipulative. As John Stott wisely cautioned, "We must be global Christians with a global vision because our God is a global God." Our use of artificial intelligence should enhance, not replace, genuine human connection and authentic community building.

Looking ahead, emerging technologies like augmented reality (AR) and virtual reality (VR) present exciting possibilities for social media evangelism. Imagine AR filters that allow users to virtually 'try on' biblical character costumes while learning about their stories or VR prayer rooms where believers from around the world can gather in a shared virtual space. As these technologies mature, artificial intelligence will play a crucial role in making them more intuitive, personalized, and impactful.

In conclusion, artificial intelligence is revolutionizing social media evangelism, providing churches with powerful tools to extend their digital reach and connect with seekers in meaningful ways. From optimizing content strategies to enabling personalized

357

interactions, these technologies offer unprecedented opportunities to share the Gospel in the digital age, all the while staying true to the unchanging message of God's love.

In our final section, we'll explore how artificial intelligence is enabling churches to personalize their evangelistic efforts, creating tailor-made pathways for individuals to encounter the life-changing truth of the Gospel.

Section 11.3: Personalizing Evangelistic Efforts

In the grand tapestry of human experience, each thread is unique, woven with individual struggles, joys, and spiritual journeys. Recognizing this, effective evangelism has always required a personal touch, a tailored approach that speaks to the heart of each individual. Artificial intelligence now offers unprecedented capabilities to personalize our evangelistic efforts, allowing us to reach people with messages that resonate deeply with their unique circumstances and spiritual needs.

Imagine a world where every seeker receives a customized pathway to faith, where the Gospel is presented in a way that addresses their specific questions, doubts, and life experiences. This is not a far-off dream but a present reality made possible by the thoughtful application of artificial intelligence in evangelism.

Cornerstone Community Church embraced this vision wholeheartedly. They implemented an artificial intelligence-driven platform that analyzed visitors' interactions with their website and social media channels. The system created detailed profiles of each individual, considering their interests, the types of content they engaged with, and the questions they asked. Based on these profiles, the church could tailor their outreach efforts, providing resources and messages that spoke directly to each person's spiritual journey.

One powerful application of personalized evangelism is in the realm of apologetics. Artificial intelligence can analyze an individual's questions and objections to faith, matching them with relevant resources, articles, or video content addressing these concerns. This targeted approach can be far more effective than a one-size-fits-all presentation of the Gospel.

Grace Baptist Church utilized this capability in its online ministry. They created an artificial intelligence-powered "Faith Explorer" tool on their website. Visitors could input their questions about Christianity, and the system would provide curated resources tailored to their specific inquiries. Whether someone was grappling with the problem of evil, questioning the historical accuracy of the Bible, or seeking evidence for the resurrection, the tool could guide them to relevant, thoughtful responses.

This personalized approach to apologetics reminds us of the words of C.S. Lewis, who said, "If you look for truth, you may find comfort in the end; if you look for comfort, you will not get either comfort or truth, only soft soap and wishful thinking to begin, and in the end, despair." By addressing people's genuine questions and doubts head-on, we demonstrate the intellectual robustness of our faith and create space for authentic spiritual growth.

Artificial intelligence also excels in creating personalized discipleship pathways. These systems can suggest tailored Bible study plans, devotional content, and growth opportunities by analyzing an individual's spiritual maturity, interests, and learning style. This level of personalization can significantly enhance the effectiveness of follow-up efforts after initial evangelistic contacts.

New Life Church implemented such a system in their new believers' program. After someone made a decision to follow Christ, they were invited to complete a simple questionnaire. The artificial intelligence system then created a customized growth plan, suggesting relevant Bible passages, connecting them with a mentor who shared similar interests or life experiences, and recommending small groups or service opportunities aligned with their gifts and passions. This personalized approach led to higher engagement rates and stronger spiritual growth among new believers.

While we tailor our approach, the core message of God's love and Christ's sacrifice must remain unchanged. Artificial intelligence should enhance, not replace, the timeless truths of Scripture.

The use of artificial intelligence in personalizing evangelistic efforts also raises important ethical considerations. There's a delicate balance between customization and manipulation. Churches must be transparent about their data usage and respect individual privacy, always prioritizing ethical considerations over mere effectiveness.

Moreover, there's a risk of over-relying on artificial intelligence and losing the human touch in evangelism. While artificial intelligence can provide valuable insights and suggestions, the work of evangelism ultimately requires human empathy, discernment, and reliance on the Holy Spirit's guidance.

Looking to the future, emerging technologies like augmented reality (AR) and virtual reality (VR) present exciting possibilities for personalized evangelism. Imagine AR apps that overlay biblical insights on to real-world situations tailored to an individual's specific struggles or questions. Or consider VR experiences that allow seekers to explore biblical narratives in immersive, personalized ways. As these technologies mature, artificial intelligence will play a crucial role in making them more intuitive and impactful.

The integration of artificial intelligence into personalized evangelistic efforts represents a new frontier in fulfilling the Great Commission. It allows us to reach individuals with unprecedented precision and relevance, creating tailored pathways for people to encounter the life-changing truth of the Gospel.

As we conclude our exploration of artificial intelligence in evangelism and outreach, we've seen how these technologies can transform our ability to reach the unreached, engage on social media, and personalize our evangelistic efforts. In the next chapter, we'll turn our attention to the exciting realm of emerging artificial intelligence technologies for ministry, discovering how these tools can help us prepare for the future of the Church in an increasingly digital world.

PART THREE

PART III: The Future of AI in Ministry

CHAPTER TWELVE

Emerging AI Technologies for Ministry

Section 12.1 Exploring New AI Innovations

The landscape of ministry is undergoing a profound transformation driven by rapid advancements in artificial intelligence. These emerging technologies offer unprecedented opportunities for churches to enhance their mission, engage their congregations in novel ways, and extend their reach far beyond traditional boundaries. As we venture into this new frontier, it's crucial to approach these innovations with a blend of excitement and discernment, always keeping our focus on how they can serve God's kingdom.

One of the most promising areas of artificial intelligence innovation for ministry is in the realm of natural language processing (NLP). This technology, which enables computers to understand, interpret, and generate human language, is opening up new possibilities for biblical study, sermon preparation, and pastoral care.

Consider the experience of Pastor David from Cornerstone Church. "We recently implemented an NLP system that can analyze vast amounts of theological texts, commentaries, and historical documents," he shares. "It's like having a team of research assistants at your fingertips. Last week, as I was preparing a sermon on the concept of grace, the system uncovered connections between Old Testament covenantal love and New Testament teachings on grace that I had never considered before. It's not replacing my study, but enhancing it in remarkable ways."

This application of NLP goes beyond simple keyword searches. These advanced systems can understand context, recognize themes, and even interpret nuanced theological concepts. They can trace the development of ideas throughout Scripture, offering pastors and bible study leaders a more comprehensive view of biblical narratives and doctrines.

Moreover, NLP is revolutionizing the way churches interact with their communities. Sophisticated chatbots powered by NLP can provide 24/7 support to church members and visitors, answering questions about faith, offering prayer resources, and even providing basic pastoral care support.

Pastor Sarah from New Life Fellowship explains their experience: "We implemented an NLP-powered chatbot on our website last year. It's been a game-changer for our outreach efforts. The bot can engage in meaningful conversations about faith, answer questions about our church, and even offer a listening ear to those going through tough times. It's not replacing our pastoral team, but it's providing a first point of contact that's available anytime, anywhere."

While these chatbots can never replace the deep, personal connection of human pastoral care, they can serve as a valuable first line of support, especially outside of regular office hours. They can also help identify when issues require human intervention, alerting pastoral staff to urgent needs.

Another exciting innovation in artificial intelligence for ministry is in the area of predictive analytics. By analyzing vast amounts of data, these systems can identify patterns and make predictions that can inform ministry decisions and strategies.

For example, predictive analytics can help churches anticipate community needs before they become critical. By analyzing trends in prayer requests, community data, and local news, churches can proactively develop outreach programs to address emerging issues.

Pastor John from Grace Community Church shares how they've used this technology: "Our predictive analytics system identified a growing trend of loneliness and isolation among young professionals in our community. We were able to launch a series of events and support groups specifically tailored to this demographic before it became a crisis. The impact has been significant – we've seen a 30% increase in young adult engagement in our church over the past six months."

This technology can also help churches optimize their resource allocation, from volunteer scheduling to budget planning. By predicting peak times for different ministries and identifying areas of greatest need, churches can ensure they're stewarding their resources effectively.

Artificial intelligence is also making waves in the realm of personalized discipleship. Advanced machine learning algorithms can analyze an individual's spiritual journey, learning style, and areas of interest to create customized growth plans.

"We've implemented an AI-driven discipleship program," says Pastor Rachel from Hillside Baptist. "It suggests Bible reading plans, devotional content, and spiritual exercises tailored to each person's unique journey. We've seen a marked increase in engagement with spiritual disciplines since implementing this system. It's like having a personal spiritual coach for every member of our congregation."

These systems can adapt in real-time based on an individual's progress and feedback, ensuring that the discipleship journey remains challenging and relevant. They can also identify when someone might be struggling or drifting away, alerting pastoral staff to reach out.

In the area of worship and music ministry, artificial intelligence is opening up new avenues for creativity and engagement. AI-powered composition tools can assist worship leaders in creating new songs or arranging existing ones to fit their congregation's needs.

Sarah, the worship leader at Crossroads Church, explains their experience: "We've been experimenting with an AI composition tool to help us write new worship songs. It analyzes the structure and themes of popular worship songs, as well as our congregation's preferences, and suggests melodic and lyrical ideas. It's not writing the songs for us, but it's sparking our creativity in new ways. Last month, we introduced a new song that was a collaborative effort between our team and the AI system. The congregation's response was overwhelmingly positive."

These AI systems can also help optimize the flow of worship services. By analyzing data on congregation engagement, they can suggest song selections and service elements that are likely to resonate most deeply with the church body.

In the realm of church administration, artificial intelligence is streamlining operations and freeing up valuable time for ministry leaders. From automated bookkeeping systems to smart donation platforms, these tools are reducing the administrative burden on church staff.

Pastor Tom from City Light Church shares, "We implemented an AI-powered administrative system last year. It's handling everything from membership database management to financial forecasting. The amount of time it's freed up for our staff to focus on relational ministry is incredible. We're able to be more efficient in our operations and more effective in our mission."

These systems can also provide valuable insights for church leadership. By analyzing trends in attendance, giving, and program participation, they can help church leaders make data-informed decisions about ministry direction and resource allocation.

Artificial intelligence is also enhancing churches' ability to provide accessibility and inclusion. Advanced speech recognition and synthesis technologies are making services more accessible to those with hearing impairments. Real-time translation services powered by AI are breaking down language barriers in multicultural congregations.

Pastor Miguel from Abundant Life Church explains, "We have a diverse congregation with members from over 20 different countries. We've started using an AI-powered translation system that provides real-time subtitles in multiple languages during our services. It's been beautiful to see people from different linguistic backgrounds worshiping together, each understanding the message in their own language."

In the realm of outreach and evangelism, artificial intelligence is providing churches with powerful tools to extend their reach. Social media algorithms can help churches target their content to those most likely to be receptive to the message. AI-powered analytics can identify trends and topics that are resonating with people, helping churches frame the gospel message in relevant and compelling ways.

Pastor David from New Hope Church shares their experience: "We've been using an AI system to help us with our social media outreach. It analyzes trending topics and suggests ways we can engage with these conversations from a faith perspective. Last month, it identified a trending discussion about finding purpose in life. We were able to create content that spoke to this search for meaning from a Christian worldview. The engagement we saw was unprecedented – our post reached over 100,000 people, and we had dozens of people reach out wanting to know more about faith."

Virtual and augmented reality, powered by artificial intelligence, are opening up new possibilities for immersive biblical experiences. Imagine being able to take a virtual tour of ancient Jerusalem as you study the life of Jesus, or using augmented reality to overlay historical and cultural information as you read your Bible.

Pastor Sarah from Truth Community Church explains how they're using this technology: "We've started incorporating VR experiences into our youth ministry. Last month, as we were studying the Exodus, our teens were able to virtually 'walk' through the parted Red Sea. The impact on their engagement with the story was remarkable. It's not replacing traditional Bible study, but it's adding a new dimension to it."

Another exciting area of innovation is in the use of artificial intelligence for mission work and global outreach. Language processing technologies are accelerating Bible translation efforts, potentially bringing the Word of God to unreached people groups faster than ever before.

Moreover, AI-powered data analysis can help mission organizations identify areas of greatest need and optimize their resource allocation. By analyzing complex data sets on global poverty, health issues, and spiritual receptivity, these systems can help guide strategic decisions about where to focus mission efforts.

As we explore these innovations, it's crucial to approach them with discernment and a strong ethical framework. The integration of artificial intelligence into ministry raises important questions about privacy, the role of human leadership, and the potential for creating digital divides within congregations.

Pastor John from Grace Community Church emphasizes this point: "As exciting as these technologies are, we always come back to our core values and mission. We ask ourselves: How does this technology help us love God and love people better? How can we use it in a way that respects the privacy and autonomy of our congregation? How do we ensure we're not excluding those who might not have access to or comfort with these technologies?"

Churches must also be mindful of the potential for over-reliance on technology. Artificial intelligence should enhance, not replace, the fundamentally relational nature of ministry. The discernment of the Holy Spirit, the wisdom of seasoned spiritual leaders, and the organic, Spirit-led nature of true ministry must always take precedence over technological capabilities.

As we look to the future, we can anticipate even more transformative applications of artificial intelligence in ministry. Advancements in brain-computer interfaces, while still in their infancy, could potentially revolutionize how we engage in prayer and meditation. Quantum computing, as it develops, could provide unprecedented capabilities for analyzing complex theological concepts and global ministry data.

However, as we embrace these innovations, we must always remember the words of the Apostle Paul in 1 Corinthians 13:1-2: "If I speak in the tongues of men or of angels, but do not have love, I am only a resounding gong or a clanging cymbal. If I have the gift of prophecy and can fathom all mysteries and all knowledge, and if I have a faith that can move mountains, but do not have love, I am nothing."

Artificial intelligence, no matter how advanced, is ultimately a tool. Its value in ministry lies not in its technological sophistication, but in how we use it to fulfill the Great Commission and live out Christ's commandment to love God and love our neighbors.

As we navigate this new frontier, let us approach it with wisdom, creativity, and unwavering faith. May our use of artificial intelligence in ministry always serve to glorify God, edify the body of Christ, and draw people into a deeper relationship with their Creator. In doing so, we can embrace the opportunities of the future while remaining rooted in the timeless truths of our faith.

The path ahead is filled with exciting possibilities for enhancing our ability to share the gospel, disciple believers, and serve our communities. As we step into this AI-enhanced future of ministry, may we always remember that our ultimate reliance is not on technology, but on the power of the Holy Spirit working through us to transform lives and advance God's kingdom.

Section 12.2 AI and the Future of Worship

The integration of artificial intelligence into worship practices heralds a new era for churches worldwide. This technological revolution promises to reshape how congregations experience and participate in worship, offering both exciting possibilities and profound challenges. As we explore this intersection of faith and innovation, we must approach it with discernment, always seeking to honor God and foster authentic spiritual experiences.

The concept of worship, at its core, remains unchanged – it is the heartfelt expression of reverence, adoration, and submission to God. However, the methods and tools we use to facilitate this worship are evolving rapidly. Artificial intelligence stands poised to transform various aspects of our worship services, from music and preaching to community engagement and accessibility.

One of the most significant ways artificial intelligence is shaping the future of worship is through personalized experiences. Advanced algorithms can analyze individual preferences, spiritual maturity levels, and engagement patterns to tailor worship elements for each congregant. Imagine walking into a church where the worship team plays songs that resonate deeply with your current spiritual state, or hearing a sermon that addresses the exact questions you've been wrestling with.

Pastor James of Hillside Community Church shares his experience with this technology: "We implemented an artificial intelligence system that analyzes congregational data to suggest worship sets and sermon topics. It's uncanny how often it identifies themes that are particularly relevant to our church body. However, we're always careful to balance these insights with prayer and spiritual discernment."

This level of personalization, while powerful, raises important questions about the communal nature of worship. The church has always been a place where diverse individuals come together as one body to worship God. How do we maintain this unity while also catering to individual needs and preferences?

John Stott, in his book "The Living Church," emphasizes the importance of corporate worship: "Christian worship is a corporate activity. It is something which, by its very nature, we do together." As churches implement personalization technologies, they must be mindful of this principle, ensuring that individualized experiences don't fragment the congregation but rather enhance the collective worship experience.

Another area where artificial intelligence is making significant inroads is in the realm of music ministry. Advanced composition algorithms can generate original worship songs, taking into account theological themes, musical styles preferred by the congregation, and even the acoustic properties of the worship space.

Sarah, the worship leader at Grace Fellowship, explains how they've incorporated this technology: "We use artificial intelligence as a collaborative tool in our songwriting process. It generates melodic ideas and lyrical phrases based on Scripture, which we then refine and develop as a team. It's opened up new creative avenues for us, but we always ensure that the final product is imbued with genuine human emotion and spiritual authenticity."

The use of artificial intelligence in worship music raises intriguing theological questions. If a song is generated by an algorithm, can it truly be a heartfelt offering to God? The answer likely lies in the intent and spirit behind its use. Just as we use instruments – themselves forms of technology – to create music for worship, artificial intelligence can be seen as another tool in service of praising God.

Preaching is another aspect of worship that stands to be transformed by artificial intelligence. Advanced natural language processing can assist pastors in sermon preparation, offering insights from vast databases of theological works, suggesting relevant illustrations, and even helping to structure the message for maximum impact.

Pastor David of New Life Church shares his perspective: "I've found artificial intelligence to be an invaluable research assistant. It helps me uncover connections in Scripture I might have missed and suggests contemporary applications for ancient truths. However, the core message always comes from my personal study and prayer. The technology enhances my preparation but doesn't replace the guidance of the Holy Spirit."

Looking ahead, we might see artificial intelligence systems that can provide real-time feedback during sermon delivery, analyzing audience engagement and suggesting on-the-fly adjustments. While this could potentially enhance the effectiveness of preaching, it also risks turning sermons into performance-driven events rather than Spirit-led proclamations of God's Word.

The challenge lies not in the technology itself, but in how we apply it in alignment with our faith and values.

Artificial intelligence also offers exciting possibilities for enhancing accessibility in worship. Real-time translation services powered by advanced language models can make services more inclusive for non-native speakers. For the hearing impaired, artificial intelligence can provide highly accurate closed captioning. Visual description algorithms can assist blind congregants in experiencing visual elements of the service.

These applications of artificial intelligence align beautifully with the biblical principle of making disciples of all nations (Matthew 28:19-20). By breaking down language and sensory barriers, we can create more inclusive worship environments that reflect the diversity of God's kingdom.

Virtual and augmented reality, powered by artificial intelligence, presents another frontier for the future of worship. Imagine donning a VR headset and finding yourself virtually transported to a beautifully rendered heavenly throne room as described in Revelation, deepening your sense of awe during worship. Or consider using augmented reality to overlay visual representations of biblical narratives as they're being preached, bringing Scripture to life in new ways.

Pastor Sarah of Cornerstone Church recently experimented with this technology: "We used augmented reality during our sermon series on the life of Jesus. As I preached, congregants could use their smartphones to see 3D renderings of the Sea of Galilee or the Temple in Jerusalem. It added a new dimension to their understanding of the biblical context."

While these immersive technologies offer exciting possibilities, they also present challenges. How do we ensure that these virtual experiences enhance rather than distract from genuine worship? How do we maintain the importance of physical gatherings when virtual attendance becomes increasingly sophisticated?

The role of artificial intelligence in fostering online communities is another important consideration for the future of worship. As churches expand their digital presence, artificial intelligence can help create more engaging and interactive online worship experiences. Chatbots can welcome virtual attendees, answer questions, and even facilitate small group discussions after the service.

However, we must be cautious not to let digital convenience undermine the biblical exhortation not to give up meeting together (Hebrews 10:25). The

challenge for churches will be to use artificial
intelligence to enhance online engagement while still
encouraging physical gathering and genuine human
connection.

As we look to the future, we can anticipate even more
transformative applications of artificial intelligence in
worship. Brain-computer interfaces, still in their
infancy, could potentially allow for more direct,
thought-based interactions during worship. Imagine
being able to visualize the prayers of the congregation
in real-time, fostering a deeper sense of corporate
intercession.

Emotion recognition technology could allow worship
spaces to respond dynamically to the collective
emotional state of the congregation, adjusting
lighting, music, or even scent to enhance the worship
atmosphere. While this might create powerful sensory
experiences, we must be careful not to manipulate
emotions or prioritize feelings over genuine spiritual
engagement.

The potential for global, real-time collaboration in worship is another exciting prospect. Artificial intelligence could facilitate simultaneous multi-site worship experiences, with churches around the world participating together, transcending geographical and cultural boundaries. This modern-day echo of Pentecost could powerfully demonstrate the global unity of the body of Christ.

As we navigate these possibilities, we must always keep in mind the words of Jesus in John 4:24: "God is spirit, and his worshipers must worship in the Spirit and in truth." No matter how advanced our technology becomes, true worship will always be a matter of the heart, guided by the Holy Spirit.

The integration of artificial intelligence into worship also raises important ethical considerations. The collection and analysis of personal data to enhance worship experiences must be balanced with respect for privacy and personal autonomy. Churches must be transparent about their use of technology and give congregants the option to participate or opt-out.

Moreover, there's a risk of creating a digital divide within congregations. Not all members may have equal access to or comfort with advanced technologies. Churches must be mindful of this and ensure that their embrace of artificial intelligence doesn't inadvertently exclude or alienate certain members of their community.

Another consideration is the environmental impact of increased technology use. As stewards of God's creation, churches must consider the energy consumption and electronic waste associated with advanced artificial intelligence systems. Finding a balance between technological advancement and environmental responsibility will be crucial.

As artificial intelligence becomes more prevalent in worship, church leaders must also grapple with deeper theological questions. How do we understand the role of human creativity and divine inspiration in an age of artificial intelligence-generated content? Can an artificial intelligence system facilitate genuine spiritual experiences, or is human intermediation always necessary?

389

These questions don't have easy answers, but wrestling with them can deepen our understanding of worship and our relationship with God. As C.S. Lewis wrote, "I believe in Christianity as I believe that the sun has risen: not only because I see it, but because by it I see everything else." Our engagement with artificial intelligence in worship should similarly illuminate our faith, helping us see God's truth more clearly.

It's also worth considering how the integration of artificial intelligence into worship might impact our understanding of church leadership roles. Will we see the emergence of "tech pastors" who specialize in leveraging artificial intelligence for ministry? How will seminary education need to adapt to prepare leaders for this new reality?

As we prepare for this AI-enhanced future of worship, it's crucial that we ground all our innovations in sound theology and timeless spiritual principles. The goal of incorporating artificial intelligence into worship should never be technological sophistication for its own sake but rather the facilitation of deeper, more meaningful encounters with God.

We must also remain mindful of the potential for over-reliance on technology. Artificial intelligence should enhance, not replace, the fundamental human and spiritual aspects of worship. The discernment of the Holy Spirit, the wisdom of seasoned spiritual leaders, and the organic, Spirit-led nature of true worship must always take precedence over technological capabilities.

In conclusion, the future of worship in an age of artificial intelligence holds both tremendous promise and significant challenges. It offers us tools to make our worship more accessible, engaging, and personalized than ever before. At the same time, it challenges us to remain true to the essence of worship as a heartfelt, Spirit-led response to God's glory.

As we move forward, let us approach this new frontier with wisdom, creativity, and unwavering faith. May our use of artificial intelligence in worship always serve to glorify God, edify the body of Christ, and draw people into a deeper relationship with their Creator. In doing so, we can embrace the opportunities of the future while remaining rooted in the timeless truths of our faith.

The journey ahead is uncharted, but it is also filled with exciting possibilities for enriching our worship experiences and expanding our ability to honor God with all of our heart, soul, mind, and strength – and now, perhaps, with our technological capabilities as well. As we navigate this new territory, may we always remember that the object of our worship – our eternal, all-knowing, all-loving God – remains unchanging, even as the methods we use to worship Him continue to evolve.

Section 12.3 Preparing for Technological Changes in Ministry

As artificial intelligence and related technologies continue to evolve rapidly, churches find themselves at a critical juncture. Preparing for technological changes in ministry has never been more pressing. This preparation involves not only acquiring new tools and skills but also cultivating a mindset of adaptability and discernment. The journey ahead requires thoughtful planning, ethical consideration, and a steadfast commitment to the church's core mission.

Developing a comprehensive technology strategy is the cornerstone of this preparation process. Churches, regardless of their size or denomination, need to assess their current capabilities, set clear objectives, and create a roadmap for implementation. This process begins with an honest evaluation of the church's existing technological infrastructure and the digital literacy of its staff and congregation.

Pastor Sarah of Grace Community Church recalls the moment she realized the need for a technology strategy. "We had bits and pieces of technology scattered throughout our ministries but no cohesive plan," she says. "It was like trying to build a house without a blueprint." Sarah and her team spent several months assessing their current systems, surveying the congregation's needs and capabilities, and researching emerging technologies. The result was a comprehensive five-year technology plan that aligned with the church's mission and values.

From this foundation, church leadership can identify specific ministry goals that technology could help achieve. These include improving communication with the congregation, enhancing worship experiences, expanding outreach efforts, or streamlining administrative tasks. The key is to focus on how technology can serve the church's mission rather than adopting technology for its own sake.

Creating a roadmap for implementation is the next crucial step. This should include timelines, budget considerations, and specific milestones. It's important to approach this as a phased process rather than attempting to overhaul everything at once. "We broke our plan into manageable chunks," Pastor Sarah explains. "We started with upgrading our church management software, then moved on to enhancing our online presence, and now we're exploring artificial intelligence tools for pastoral care."

Hand in hand with strategy development is the cultivation of digital literacy among church leaders, staff, and congregants. This is not a one-time effort but an ongoing process of learning and adaptation. Churches might implement regular training sessions, create mentorship opportunities, and develop a resource library to support continuous learning.

Pastor John of Cornerstone Baptist Church found that fostering digital literacy was one of his biggest challenges. "Many of our older members were intimidated by technology," he says. "We had to approach this with patience and understanding." Cornerstone implemented a "Tech Buddies" program, pairing tech-savvy youth with older members for one-on-one training sessions. "It not only improved digital literacy but also strengthened intergenerational relationships in our church," Pastor John notes.

The goal of these efforts is not to create technology experts but to ensure that everyone in the church community feels comfortable and confident in using the tools that will increasingly become part of ministry life. This might involve workshops on using church management software, social media platforms, or basic artificial intelligence tools. It's also important to provide resources for self-paced learning, recognizing that people have different learning styles and schedules.

As churches adopt new technologies, they must also develop robust ethical frameworks to guide their use. This is perhaps one of the most critical aspects of preparing for technological change in ministry. The rapid advancement of artificial intelligence, in particular, raises complex ethical questions that churches must grapple with.

Forming an ethics committee is an excellent first step. This committee should be comprised of church leaders, tech experts, and ethicists who can provide diverse perspectives on the implications of new technologies. Clear guidelines should be established for the use of artificial intelligence and other technologies in various ministry contexts, addressing issues like data privacy, transparency, and the balance between technological efficiency and human touch.

Pastor David of New Life Church shares his experience: "When we first started using artificial intelligence for pastoral care support, we realized we were entering uncharted ethical territory. We had to ask ourselves hard questions about privacy, the role of human pastors, and how to ensure that our use of technology aligns with our theological beliefs." New Life Church developed a comprehensive ethical framework that is now reviewed and updated annually to keep pace with technological advancements.

These guidelines should be regularly reviewed and updated as technologies evolve and new ethical considerations arise. It's also important to communicate these guidelines clearly to the congregation, fostering transparency and trust in the church's use of technology.

While embracing innovation, churches must also maintain a delicate balance with their spiritual foundations and traditions. This requires ongoing theological reflection on the role of technology in ministry, considering how new tools align with or challenge traditional understandings of worship, community, and discipleship.

John Stott, in his book "The Contemporary Christian," emphasizes the importance of being "contemporary without being conformist." This principle applies aptly to the integration of technology in ministry. Churches must find ways to leverage new tools while staying true to their core beliefs and practices.

It's crucial to identify core spiritual practices that should remain technology-free, preserving sacred spaces and times for unmediated communion with God and fellow believers. This might include certain prayer times, retreats, or communion services. The goal is not to reject technology wholesale but to use it judiciously and intentionally.

Pastor Maria of Hillside Chapel shares her approach: "We've embraced technology in many aspects of our ministry, but we've also designated our Wednesday night prayer meetings as a 'tech-free zone.' It's a time for our community to unplug and focus solely on connecting with God and each other."

Church leaders must develop the capacity to adapt to rapid technological change while maintaining a strong spiritual focus. This involves continuous learning about emerging technologies, cultivating discernment in their adoption and implementation, and fostering a culture open to experimentation.

Pastor Tom of City Light Church emphasizes the importance of this adaptive mindset: "We've had to learn to be comfortable with discomfort," he says. "Technology is changing so rapidly that by the time you feel you've mastered one tool, three new ones have emerged. We've had to cultivate a spirit of continuous learning and adaptability."

This adaptability extends to viewing failures not as setbacks but as valuable learning opportunities. When City Light Church's first attempt at live streaming services encountered technical difficulties, Pastor Tom used it as a chance to involve more volunteers in the tech ministry and to refine their processes. "Each hiccup taught us something new," he reflects.

To support new technologies, churches need to invest in robust digital infrastructure. This involves regularly assessing and upgrading hardware and software capabilities, considering cloud integration for greater flexibility, and implementing strong cybersecurity measures to protect sensitive data and maintain trust with the congregation.

Pastor Sarah of Grace Community Church learned the importance of this the hard way. "We thought our systems were secure, but a data breach taught us otherwise," she shares. "Now, we work with cybersecurity experts to ensure our digital infrastructure is as robust as possible. It's an ongoing process, but it's crucial for maintaining the trust of our congregation."

As ministry increasingly extends into digital spaces, churches must learn to foster genuine community in these environments. This might involve developing strategies for online small groups, creating digital discipleship programs that leverage artificial intelligence for personalized spiritual growth journeys, or establishing virtual prayer rooms where people can gather for intercession and support regardless of physical location.

Pastor John of Cornerstone Baptist Church has been experimenting with digital community-building. "We've created a virtual coffee hour after our online services," he explains. "It's a space where people can chat, pray together, and form connections. It's different from in-person fellowship, but it's been a lifeline for our members who can't attend physically, especially during the pandemic."

The future of ministry likely involves a hybrid of in-person and digital experiences. Churches should prepare by designing flexible worship spaces that can accommodate both physical and virtual participants, implementing integrated communication systems, and providing training for staff and volunteers on effectively ministering in hybrid environments.

Pastor David of New Life Church shares his vision: "We're redesigning our sanctuary to include areas for camera setups and screens that allow in-person and online attendees to interact. We're also training our greeters to welcome both physical and virtual attendees. It's a new frontier, but it's exciting to see how it can expand our reach."

While we can't predict the future with certainty, churches can prepare by staying informed about emerging trends. This might involve assigning team members to monitor new technologies, engaging in scenario planning exercises, or forming partnerships with technology companies to pilot new tools and shape their development for ministry applications.

Pastor Maria of Hillside Chapel has taken this approach to heart. "We've formed a 'Future of Ministry' task force," she explains. "Their job is to keep an eye on emerging technologies and consider how they might impact our ministry. They've helped us stay ahead of the curve and be proactive rather than reactive in our approach to technology."

As churches embrace new technologies, they must be mindful not to exclude those with limited access to technological literacy. Addressing this digital divide is a crucial aspect of preparing for technological changes in ministry. It might involve providing devices or internet access to members who can't afford them, ensuring that key aspects of church life remain accessible through non-digital means, and implementing programs to help less tech-savvy members learn to use new tools and platforms.

Pastor Tom of City Light Church shares his experience: "We realized that our shift to more digital ministry was unintentionally excluding some of our elderly members and those from lower-income backgrounds. We started a 'Tech Equity' initiative, providing refurbished devices and internet hotspots to those who needed them. We also make sure to offer phone and mail options for key communications."

Amidst rapid technological change, cultivating spiritual discernment has become more crucial than ever. Churches should create spaces for prayer and reflection on technology use, encourage open dialogue about the impacts of new tools on spiritual life, and continually ground all technological decisions in the church's mission and values.

Pastor Sarah of Grace Community Church emphasizes this point: "We've incorporated discussions about technology and faith into our small group curriculum. It's important that our congregation doesn't just use these tools blindly, but thinks critically about how they impact our walk with God and our community."

Financial considerations are another crucial aspect of preparing for technological changes in ministry. Implementing new technologies often requires significant investment, both in terms of hardware and software, and in terms of training and support. Churches need to develop strategic budgeting practices that allow for these investments while maintaining financial stability.

Pastor John of Cornerstone Baptist Church shares his approach: "We've started setting aside a 'Technology Tithe' - 10% of our annual budget dedicated to technological upgrades and training. It ensures we're always moving forward, but in a way that's financially sustainable for our church."

It's also important to consider the potential return on investment for technological implementations. While the spiritual impact of ministry can't always be quantified, churches can track metrics like engagement levels, outreach effectiveness, and operational efficiency to gauge the impact of their technological investments.

As churches navigate this technological frontier, it's crucial to maintain a focus on the human element of ministry. Technology should enhance, not replace, human connections and pastoral care. Pastor David of New Life Church reflects on this balance: "We use artificial intelligence to help us identify pastoral care needs, but the actual care is always provided by human pastors. Technology is a tool to help us be more effective in our human ministry, not a replacement for it."

In all these preparations, churches must remember that the goal is not technological sophistication for its own sake but more effective ministry and discipleship. Every technological decision should be made with the question: How does this help us fulfill our mission of sharing God's love and making disciples?

Pastor Maria of Hillside Chapel sums it up well: "At the end of the day, our call is to love God and love people. Technology is just a tool to help us do that more effectively in today's world. We need to be wise in how we use it, always keeping our focus on Christ and His mission for the church."

In navigating this technological frontier, churches would do well to remember the words of C.S. Lewis: "God is no fonder of intellectual slackers than of any other slackers. If you are thinking of becoming a Christian, I warn you, you are embarking on something which is going to take the whole of you, brains and all." Preparing for technological changes in ministry requires the engagement of our full faculties - intellectual, spiritual, and practical - as we seek to faithfully steward these new tools for the advancement of God's kingdom.

As we look to the future, it's clear that the landscape of ministry will continue to evolve with technological advancements. Churches that proactively prepare for these changes, grounding their approach in sound strategy, ethical consideration, and spiritual discernment, will be well-positioned to leverage these tools for greater kingdom impact. The key is to remain flexible, continuously learning, and always focused on the timeless mission of the church in a rapidly changing world.

CHAPTER THIRTEEN

Ethical and Theological Implications

Section 13.1 Navigating the Ethical Dilemmas of AI

The dawn of artificial intelligence in ministry brings with it a host of ethical considerations that church leaders must navigate with wisdom and discernment. As we stand on the precipice of this technological revolution, we find ourselves grappling with questions that challenge our understanding of pastoral care, privacy, and even the nature of spiritual guidance itself.

Pastor James of Cornerstone Community Church leaned back in his chair, his brow furrowed in contemplation. The artificial intelligence system his church had implemented to assist with pastoral care had just flagged a potential crisis situation. A long-time member's online activity and giving patterns had suddenly changed, indicating possible financial distress or personal upheaval. The system suggested immediate intervention.

"On one hand," Pastor James mused, "this technology allows us to be more proactive in caring for our flock. On the other, are we crossing a line by monitoring our members so closely?"

This scenario encapsulates one of the core ethical dilemmas churches face as they integrate artificial intelligence into their ministries: the balance between enhanced care and potential invasion of privacy. The ability to analyze vast amounts of data to identify needs within the congregation is powerful. Still, it also raises questions about consent, transparency, and the appropriate use of personal information.

In his book Issues Facing Christians Today, John Stott reminds us that "the Christian mind is the prerequisite of Christian thinking. And Christian thinking is the prerequisite of Christian action." As we confront these ethical challenges, we must engage our minds fully, grounding our decisions in biblical principles and thoughtfully considering their implications.

Another ethical consideration arises from the use of artificial intelligence in spiritual guidance and counseling. Many churches have implemented chatbots or virtual assistants to provide 24/7 support to their members. While these tools can offer comfort and biblical wisdom at any hour, they also raise questions about the nature of pastoral care and the role of human ministers.

Pastor Sarah of New Life Fellowship shared her experience: "Our artificial intelligence-powered chatbot has been a tremendous resource, especially for those struggling with anxiety or loneliness in the middle of the night. But we've had to be very clear about its limitations. It's a first point of contact, not a replacement for human pastoral care."

The challenge here lies in striking the right balance. Artificial intelligence can provide valuable support and resources, but it lacks the empathy, discernment, and ability to listen that are hallmarks of effective pastoral care. Churches must be careful not to create a false equivalence between artificial intelligence-driven interactions and genuine human ministry.

These concerns might tempt us to take the easy path to either wholesale reject these new technologies or to embrace them uncritically. The difficult but necessary approach is to thoughtfully engage with them, carefully considering their ethical implications and how they align with our calling as ministers of the Gospel.

One of the most pressing ethical concerns surrounding artificial intelligence in ministry is the potential for bias and discrimination. Artificial intelligence systems are only as unbiased as the data they're trained on and the people who design them. If not carefully developed and monitored, these systems could perpetuate or even amplify existing biases within our churches and communities.

For instance, an artificial intelligence system used for outreach planning might inadvertently favor certain demographics based on historical data, potentially neglecting underserved groups within the community. Church leaders must be vigilant in examining the outputs and recommendations of their artificial intelligence systems, always asking whether they align with the church's mission to minister to all people equally.

The use of artificial intelligence in sermon preparation and delivery also presents ethical challenges. While these tools can provide valuable insights and help pastors connect Scripture to current events, there's a risk of over-reliance on technology at the expense of personal study and Holy Spirit-led discernment.

Pastor David of Grace Community Church reflected on this tension: "I've found our artificial intelligence research tool incredibly helpful in uncovering new perspectives on familiar passages. But I have to constantly remind myself that it's a tool, not a replacement for prayer and personal engagement with God's Word."

The ethical use of artificial intelligence in this context requires a deep commitment to authenticity and transparency. Pastors should be open with their congregations about how they use these tools, always emphasizing that the core message comes from their personal study and the leading of the Holy Spirit.

Another ethical consideration is the potential for artificial intelligence to create or exacerbate digital divides within congregations. As churches increasingly rely on technology for communication, discipleship, and even worship, there's a risk of inadvertently marginalizing those who lack access to or comfort with these tools.

In his book The Local Church Today, Bill Scheidler emphasizes the importance of the church as a place for all believers. This principle must guide our implementation of artificial intelligence, ensuring that our use of technology enhances rather than hinders our ability to minister to everyone in our communities.

As we navigate these ethical dilemmas, it's crucial to develop robust frameworks for decision-making. This involves not only understanding the capabilities and limitations of artificial intelligence but also deepening our theological reflection on issues of human dignity, free will, and the nature of spiritual growth.

C.S. Lewis, in his book "Mere Christianity," writes, "God has not been trying an experiment on my faith or love in order to find out their quality. He knew it already. It was I who didn't." This reminder of God's omniscience and our limited understanding should instill in us a sense of humility as we grapple with the ethical implications of artificial intelligence in ministry.

Looking ahead, the ethical challenges surrounding artificial intelligence in ministry will only grow more complex. As these systems become more advanced, we may find ourselves wrestling with questions about the nature of consciousness, the boundaries of human-machine interaction in spiritual contexts, and the role of artificial intelligence in discerning God's will.

Church leaders must commit to ongoing education and dialogue to navigate these waters. This involves not only staying informed about technological advancements but also fostering conversations within our congregations about the ethical use of these tools. By engaging our communities in these discussions, we can develop collective wisdom and ensure that our use of artificial intelligence aligns with our values and mission.

Moreover, churches should consider developing ethical guidelines or covenants for their use of artificial intelligence. These documents can serve as touchstones, helping leaders make consistent, principled decisions as they implement new technologies.

As we conclude our exploration of the ethical dilemmas surrounding artificial intelligence in ministry, we find ourselves standing at the intersection of tremendous opportunity and significant responsibility. The power of these tools to enhance our ministry efforts is undeniable, but so too is their potential for misuse or unintended negative consequences.

In the face of these challenges, we must return to the fundamental truths of our faith. Our ultimate allegiance is not to technological progress but to the unchanging God who calls us to love Him and our neighbors. As we harness the power of artificial intelligence, may we do so with wisdom, integrity, and an unwavering commitment to the Gospel.

The ethical use of artificial intelligence in ministry is not a destination but a journey - one that requires constant vigilance, thoughtful reflection, and a willingness to course-correct as we learn and grow. As we embark on this journey, may we be guided by the words of the prophet Micah: "He has shown you, O mortal, what is good. And what does the Lord require of you? To act justly and to love mercy and to walk humbly with your God" (Micah 6:8).

In our next section, we'll explore how artificial intelligence is reshaping our understanding of free will and divine sovereignty - age-old theological questions that take on new dimensions in the age of intelligent machines. As we delve into these profound topics, we'll seek to ground our reflections in Scripture and the wisdom of those who have gone before us, always striving to honor God in our use of these powerful new tools.

Section 13.2 AI and Free Will: A Theological Discussion

Integrating artificial intelligence into ministry practices inevitably leads us to grapple with profound theological questions, particularly concerning the nature of free will and God's sovereignty. As we stand at the crossroads of faith and technology, we find ourselves revisiting age-old debates with fresh perspectives and new challenges.

Pastor Thomas of Hillside Baptist Church sat in his study, pondering the implications of the church's new artificial intelligence-powered discipleship program. The system had just suggested a personalized spiritual growth plan for a young member struggling with doubt. "Is this truly Spirit-led guidance," he wondered, "or are we reducing the mystery of faith to algorithms?"

This scenario encapsulates a central tension in the artificial intelligence era: the interplay between human choice, divine guidance, and technological influence. As artificial intelligence systems become more sophisticated in predicting behavior and offering personalized recommendations, we must carefully consider how this impacts our understanding of free will and spiritual discernment.

C.S. Lewis, in his seminal work "Mere Christianity," writes, "God created things which had free will. That means creatures which can go either wrong or right." This foundational Christian belief in human free will seems challenged by the deterministic nature of artificial intelligence algorithms. If our choices can be predicted and influenced by machines, what does this mean for our moral responsibility and our relationship with God?

To navigate this complex terrain, we must first recognize that the concept of free will has always existed in tension with our understanding of God's sovereignty. The Apostle Paul grapples with this paradox in Romans 9:19-21, using the metaphor of the potter and the clay to illustrate God's authority over His creation. The introduction of artificial intelligence adds another layer to this theological puzzle.

Consider the use of artificial intelligence in personalized Bible study recommendations. These systems analyze our reading habits, engagement patterns, and even our emotional responses to suggest Scripture passages tailored to our current spiritual state. On one hand, this can be seen as a powerful tool for deepening our engagement with God's Word. On the other hand, it raises questions about the role of human agency and divine guidance in our spiritual journey.

Pastor Sarah of New Life Fellowship shared her perspective: "We've found our artificial intelligence Bible study tool to be incredibly helpful in guiding new believers through Scripture. But we always emphasize that these are suggestions, not mandates. The Holy Spirit remains our ultimate guide in understanding God's Word."

This approach acknowledges the utility of artificial intelligence while affirming the primacy of divine guidance and human discernment. It recognizes that while artificial intelligence can provide valuable insights, the deeply personal nature of faith requires active engagement and choice on the part of the believer.

John Stott, in his book "Basic Christianity," reminds us that "God's sovereignty does not diminish man's responsibility." This principle takes on new relevance in the age of artificial intelligence. Even as these systems become more adept at predicting and influencing human behavior, we must maintain a firm belief in moral agency and personal accountability.

The use of artificial intelligence in pastoral care presents another arena where questions of free will and divine guidance come to the fore. Many churches now employ artificial intelligence systems to analyze congregational data and flag potential pastoral needs. While this can enable more proactive ministry, it also raises questions about the nature of spiritual discernment and the role of human intuition in pastoral care.

Pastor David of Grace Community Church reflected on this challenge: "Our artificial intelligence system recently flagged a member as potentially being at risk for depression based on their online activity and giving patterns. It prompted me to reach out, and indeed, the member was going through a difficult time. But I can't help wondering: would the Holy Spirit have led me to this person anyway? Are we short-circuiting the spiritual aspects of pastoral care?"

This scenario highlights the delicate balance between leveraging technology to enhance our ministry efforts and maintaining our reliance on spiritual discernment. It challenges us to consider how artificial intelligence might complement, rather than replace, the God-given gifts of empathy, intuition, and Spirit-led guidance in pastoral care.

As we consider the implications of artificial intelligence for our understanding of free will, we must also grapple with questions of human uniqueness and the image of God. Genesis 1:27 tells us that God created humans in His own image. How does the increasing sophistication of artificial intelligence impact our understanding of what it means to be uniquely human?

As artificial intelligence systems become more advanced, potentially exhibiting traits we once considered uniquely human, it becomes increasingly important to ground our sense of worth and purpose in our relationship with God rather than in our cognitive capabilities.

Looking ahead, we can anticipate even more complex theological questions arising from advancements in artificial intelligence. As these systems become more sophisticated in their ability to process language, recognize emotions, and even engage in creative tasks, we may find ourselves grappling with questions about the nature of consciousness, the boundaries of personhood, and the ethical implications of creating entities that might be considered sentient.

These questions are not merely academic exercises but have practical implications for ministry. How do we approach evangelism and discipleship in a world where humans increasingly interact with artificial intelligence systems? How do we maintain the centrality of human relationship and community in an age of AI-mediated interactions?

Pastor Rachel of Cornerstone Church shared her approach: "We've started incorporating discussions about technology and faith into our youth ministry curriculum. We want our young people to think critically about how their use of AI-powered tools impacts their faith journey and their understanding of free will and God's guidance."

This proactive approach recognizes that as artificial intelligence becomes more pervasive in our daily lives, it's crucial to develop a theological framework for engaging with these technologies. It encourages believers to think deeply about how their faith informs their use of technology, rather than allowing technology to unconsciously shape their faith.

As we navigate these complex theological waters, it's crucial to maintain a posture of humility and openness to God's guidance. The Apostle Paul reminds us in 1 Corinthians 13:12, "For now we see only a reflection as in a mirror; then we shall see face to face. Now I know in part; then I shall know fully, even as I am fully known." This verse takes on new meaning in the age of artificial intelligence, reminding us of the limits of human (and machine) knowledge and the ultimate sovereignty of God.

In conclusion, the intersection of artificial intelligence and free will presents both challenges and opportunities for theological reflection and practical ministry. As we integrate these powerful tools into our church practices, we must do so thoughtfully, always grounding our approach in Scripture and maintaining a firm commitment to the dignity of human choice and the guidance of the Holy Spirit.

The questions we face are complex, and the answers may not always be clear-cut. But by engaging in thoughtful dialogue, maintaining a posture of humility, and continually seeking God's wisdom, we can navigate this new frontier in a way that honors our Creator and furthers the mission of the Church.

\

As we move forward, let us hold fast to the truth that while artificial intelligence may augment our capabilities, it does not alter our fundamental identity as bearers of God's image, called to freely choose to love and serve Him. In our next section, we'll explore how artificial intelligence is reshaping our understanding of human touch in ministry, examining both the opportunities and challenges this presents for pastoral care and community building in the digital age.

Section 13.3 The Role of Human Touch in an AI-Driven Ministry

In the bustling heart of Silicon Valley, Pastor Mark stood before his congregation at TechFaith Community Church. The sanctuary hummed with the latest artificial intelligence-enhanced systems, from personalized scripture displays to real-time sermon translation. Yet, as he gazed upon the faces before him—some physically present, others joining via high-definition holograms—he couldn't shake a nagging question: In this world of technological marvels, what role does human touch play in ministry?

This scene, while futuristic, is not far from reality for many churches embracing artificial intelligence. As we navigate this new landscape, we must grapple with the irreplaceable value of human connection in a world increasingly mediated by intelligent machines.

The essence of ministry has always been relational. Jesus modeled a personal touch ministry, from laying hands on the sick to breaking bread with his disciples. In John 13:34-35, He commands, "A new command I give you: Love one another. As I have loved you, so you must love one another. By this, everyone will know that you are my disciples if you love one another." This love, in its fullest expression, often involves physical presence and human interaction.

427

Yet, as artificial intelligence reshapes our ministry landscape, we find ourselves asking: Can the warmth of human touch be replicated or enhanced by technology? Should it be?

Pastor Sarah of New Life Fellowship shared her experience: "Our artificial intelligence pastoral care system is incredibly efficient. It can identify potential crisis situations and suggest intervention strategies with remarkable accuracy. But there's something it can't do—hold the hand of a grieving widow or embrace a celebrating new believer. Those moments of human connection are irreplaceable."

This sentiment echoes the words of John Stott, who wrote in his book "The Contemporary Christian," "The Christian faith is not just a philosophy of life or a moral code, but a living relationship with the living God." This relationship, Stott argues, is best nurtured in community with other believers.

As we integrate artificial intelligence into our ministries, we must be careful not to sacrifice the communal aspects of faith on the altar of efficiency. While artificial intelligence can enhance our ability to meet practical needs and disseminate information, it cannot fully replicate the empathy, intuition, and shared experience that form the bedrock of Christian fellowship.

Consider the practice of prayer. Many churches have implemented artificial intelligence systems that can generate personalized prayer prompts or even offer pre-written prayers based on an individual's circumstances. While these tools can be valuable aids in developing a consistent prayer life, they risk reducing prayer to a formulaic exercise rather than a heartfelt conversation with God.

Pastor David of Grace Community Church reflected on this challenge: "We introduced an artificial intelligence prayer assistant last year. It's been helpful in many ways, especially for new believers learning to articulate their prayers. But we've had to be intentional about emphasizing that prayer is fundamentally about relationship, not just saying the right words."

This tension between technological assistance and authentic spiritual practice is at the heart of many discussions about artificial intelligence in ministry. How do we leverage these powerful tools without losing the essence of what it means to be the Church—a community of believers united in Christ?

C.S. Lewis, in his book "The Four Loves," writes, "To love at all is to be vulnerable." This vulnerability, this willingness to open ourselves to others, is a crucial aspect of Christian community that cannot be fully replicated by artificial intelligence. While AI systems can facilitate connections and provide support, they cannot experience the mutual vulnerability that deepens human relationships and fosters spiritual growth.

As we navigate this new terrain, we must be mindful of the potential for artificial intelligence to create a false sense of connection. The ease of digital interaction, enhanced by intelligent systems that can mimic empathy and understanding, might lead some to neglect the more challenging but ultimately more rewarding work of building face-to-face relationships within their church community.

Pastor Rachel of Hillside Baptist shared her concerns: "We've noticed that some of our members, especially younger ones, are more comfortable interacting with our AI chatbot than with human leaders. It's efficient, always available, and never judges. But it also never challenges them to grow beyond their comfort zone in the way that real relationships do."

This observation highlights a crucial aspect of human touch in ministry—its ability to challenge and transform us. Real human interactions, with all their messiness and unpredictability, play a vital role in our spiritual formation. They teach us patience, forgiveness, and sacrificial love in ways that even the most advanced artificial intelligence system cannot.

In the context of AI-driven ministry, we must be careful not to opt for technological solutions simply because they are easier or more convenient than the often difficult work of building genuine community.

However, it would be a mistake to view artificial intelligence and human touch as entirely at odds. When thoughtfully integrated, AI can actually enhance our ability to provide meaningful human connection in ministry.

For example, artificial intelligence systems can help identify individuals in the congregation who might be feeling isolated or struggling with their faith. By analyzing patterns in attendance, online engagement, and other data points, these systems can alert pastoral staff to potential needs that might otherwise go unnoticed.

Pastor Mark of TechFaith Community Church explained their approach: "Our AI system recently flagged a member who had stopped engaging with our online content and hadn't attended services in several weeks. This prompted me to reach out personally. It turned out he was going through a crisis of faith and had been hesitant to talk about it. That human connection, facilitated by AI, made all the difference."

This example illustrates how artificial intelligence can serve as a tool to enhance, rather than replace, human touch in ministry. By handling routine tasks and providing data-driven insights, AI can free up church leaders to focus more of their time and energy on personal interactions and relationship-building.

Another area where artificial intelligence is reshaping our understanding of human touch in ministry is in the realm of global missions and cross-cultural outreach. Language barriers have long been a challenge in spreading the Gospel across cultures. While human translators provide invaluable cultural context and nuance, they are not always available or affordable for every interaction.

Artificial intelligence-powered translation tools are bridging this gap, allowing for real-time communication across language barriers. This technology enables missionaries and church leaders to connect more directly with people from different linguistic backgrounds, fostering a sense of immediate human connection that was previously challenging to achieve.

Pastor Sarah, who leads her church's global missions program, shared her experience: "We've been using AI translation in our video calls with our partner church in rural China. It's not perfect, but it allows for a level of direct, personal communication that we've never had before. You can see the joy on people's faces when they realize they can understand each other directly, without an intermediary."

While this technology certainly doesn't replace the need for cultural understanding and human translators in many contexts, it does open up new possibilities for global Christian fellowship and collaboration. It allows for more frequent, spontaneous interactions that can help build stronger relationships across cultural and linguistic divides.

However, as we embrace these technological aids to human connection, we must remain mindful of their limitations. Artificial intelligence, no matter how advanced, cannot fully capture the cultural nuances, non-verbal cues, and emotional subtleties that are crucial in human communication. There will always be a need for human wisdom and cultural sensitivity in cross-cultural ministry.

The role of human touch becomes particularly crucial when we consider pastoral care in times of crisis or grief. While artificial intelligence systems can provide valuable support—offering resources, suggesting coping strategies, or even providing a listening ear through chatbots—they cannot provide the depth of empathy and shared humanity that is often needed in our darkest hours.

Pastor John of Cornerstone Church reflected on a recent experience: "I was called to the hospital to be with a family whose child was critically ill. No amount of artificial intelligence could have replaced the simple act of sitting with them, praying together, and sharing in their pain. In those moments, the ministry of presence is irreplaceable."

This "ministry of presence" is a fundamental aspect of pastoral care that artificial intelligence cannot fully replicate. The power of silent companionship, a comforting touch, or tears shared in empathy are uniquely human expressions of God's love and care.

As we look to the future, we can anticipate that artificial intelligence will continue to evolve, potentially becoming even more sophisticated in its ability to mimic human interaction. This progression will likely bring new challenges and opportunities for ministry.

We may see the development of more advanced virtual reality systems that allow for more immersive remote interactions. While these could provide valuable connections for those unable to physically attend church due to distance or health issues, we must be cautious about seeing them as equivalent to in-person fellowship.

Bill Scheidler, in his book "The Local Church Today," emphasizes the importance of the church as a physical gathering of believers. As we integrate more virtual and AI-enhanced interactions into our ministry, we must strive to maintain the centrality of physical gathering and face-to-face community as core aspects of church life.

One potential area where artificial intelligence might enhance human touch in ministry is in helping church leaders be more intentional and effective in their relationship-building efforts. AI systems could analyze patterns of interaction within the congregation, identifying individuals who might be feeling marginalized or disconnected. This information could guide church leaders in their efforts to ensure that every member feels seen, valued, and integrated into the community.

Pastor Rachel shared how this works in her church: "Our AI system helps us track engagement across various church activities. Recently, it identified a pattern of young adults dropping out of small groups after a few months. This led us to have focused conversations with this demographic, which revealed a need for more life-stage specific groups. We would have eventually noticed this trend, but the AI helped us address it much more quickly."

This use of artificial intelligence doesn't replace the need for human discernment and relational skills, but it can help leaders be more strategic and timely in their relationship-building efforts.

As we navigate this new frontier of AI-enhanced ministry, it's crucial that we continually reflect on and reaffirm the central role of human touch. This means not only preserving spaces for unmediated human interaction but also being intentional about teaching the value of physical presence and face-to-face community, especially to younger generations who may be more comfortable with digital interactions.

Pastor Mark of TechFaith Community Church shared their approach: "We've started a 'Digital Sabbath' program, encouraging our members to set aside time each week to unplug from technology and engage in face-to-face fellowship. It's been challenging for some, but we've seen real growth in our community as a result."

Initiatives like this can help ensure that as we embrace the benefits of artificial intelligence in ministry, we don't lose sight of the irreplaceable value of human touch and physical presence.

In conclusion, as we stand at this intersection of high-tech ministry and timeless human needs, we must strive to leverage artificial intelligence in ways that enhance, rather than replace, human touch in ministry. The goal should always be to use these tools to facilitate deeper, more meaningful human connections and to create space for the kind of vulnerable, transformative relationships that are at the heart of Christian community.

As we move forward into this AI-enhanced future of ministry, may we always remember the words of the Apostle Paul in 1 Thessalonians 2:8: "So we cared for you. Because we loved you so much, we were delighted to share with you not only the gospel of God but our lives as well." This sharing of lives—messy, imperfect, and beautifully human—remains the essence of Christian ministry, no matter how advanced our technological tools become.

In our next chapter, we'll explore practical strategies for implementing artificial intelligence in your church context, offering guidance on how to navigate the challenges and opportunities we've discussed. As we delve into these practical applications, we'll continue to ground our approach in the timeless truths of Scripture and the wisdom of those who have gone before us in the faith.

CHAPTER FOURTEEN

Building an AI-Driven Ministry

Section 14.1 Practical Steps to Implementing AI in Your Church

Artificial intelligence (AI) is transforming numerous sectors and churches are beginning to realize the potential it holds for ministry. AI's future in the church is exciting, but implementing it in a way that aligns with a church's spiritual mission requires careful thought, planning, and execution. AI tools can offer tremendous benefits in terms of operational efficiency, pastoral care, evangelism, and discipleship. However, successful implementation starts with a clear, purposeful approach.

This section will walk church leaders through the key steps to practically integrate AI into their ministries, ensuring it advances both the Kingdom of God and the logistical needs of their congregations.

Understanding the Role of AI in Ministry

Before discussing specific steps for integrating AI, it is important to understand the overall role AI should play in ministry. AI, by itself, is neither inherently good nor bad. It is a powerful tool that can help churches accomplish tasks more efficiently. But it should never replace the church's core mission, which is to build relationships, disciple believers, and share the gospel.

AI excels in areas like data processing, communication, and logistical coordination, freeing up human resources for more direct spiritual engagement. It can also be used to enhance outreach by tailoring messages to specific audiences or helping manage large-scale community efforts. However, AI should be viewed as a complementary tool, aiding human efforts, rather than replacing the deep, personal connections that are essential in ministry.

Understanding this balance will help you navigate the choices ahead and ensure that AI serves your church's mission without compromising your values.

Step 1: Assess Your Church's Needs and Challenges

Every church is unique, and its needs and challenges are just as distinct. Before considering any AI implementation, conducting an internal assessment is vital. Church leaders need to ask hard questions: Where are we currently struggling? How are we using our time and resources? What specific areas of ministry could benefit from automation or technological enhancement?

Many churches face challenges in areas such as administration, outreach, and member engagement. Others may struggle with managing volunteer coordination or maintaining consistent communication with congregants. AI can assist with these issues, but it's essential to pinpoint the specific challenges your church faces so that you can choose the most beneficial AI tools.

For instance, a church with a large congregation may benefit from AI-driven church management software that automates administrative tasks such as membership tracking, scheduling, or tithing records. A smaller congregation might need AI to help improve

443

outreach, perhaps by using AI-driven social media strategies or automated newsletters to engage the local community.

Step 2: Define Clear Goals for AI Implementation

Once the church's needs are identified, the next step is to establish clear, measurable goals for how AI will be used. AI is a powerful tool, but if its implementation lacks direction, it can become a distraction rather than an aid.

Start by determining specific goals related to your identified needs. For example, if the church struggles with member retention, one goal could be to improve engagement through personalized follow-ups or AI-driven small-group recommendations. If administrative burdens are overwhelming, a goal could be to reduce the time staff spends on scheduling and record-keeping by 50%.

Defining goals not only provides direction but also allows you to measure the success of AI integration. This step will help you avoid the temptation to use technology simply for the sake of innovation, ensuring that it is always aligned with the church's mission.

Step 3: Begin with Proven AI Tools

Starting small is key to a smooth AI transition. While the capabilities of AI are vast, jumping into complex systems can overwhelm staff and leadership. Instead, begin with established, proven tools that address specific areas of need.

For example, many churches start by adopting AI-powered church management systems (CMS). These platforms can streamline member data management, volunteer coordination, event planning, and financial administration. By automating these processes, church staff and leaders can shift their focus to more personal aspects of ministry, such as pastoral care or teaching.

AI chatbots are another practical, beginner-friendly tool. Chatbots can be used to manage routine communication with congregants, answering basic questions about service times, prayer requests, and upcoming events, while also providing support for administrative tasks. Implementing a chatbot frees up church staff to focus on tasks that require personal engagement.

Similarly, sermon preparation can be enhanced by AI tools that assist with scripture research, provide historical context, and generate sermon ideas based on biblical themes. AI-driven research platforms offer pastors valuable resources quickly, allowing them to focus on delivering meaningful messages rather than spending hours gathering information.

By starting with tools that are well-established and user-friendly, your church can smoothly integrate AI without overwhelming staff or requiring drastic changes to existing systems.

Step 4: Train Your Team on New AI Tools

Implementing AI effectively requires your church staff and volunteers to become comfortable with new technologies. Training is crucial, not only for those managing administrative tasks but also for those involved in outreach, discipleship, and communication.

The first step in training your team is to offer comprehensive education on how AI works and its specific applications within your church. While AI may seem intimidating to some, it is important to demystify the technology and provide clear, practical training on its benefits.

Workshops or online courses can be useful for helping staff understand AI's potential and its limitations. Hands-on experience will make AI tools more approachable and demonstrate their real-world applications. Providing step-by-step guidance, instructional videos, and ongoing technical support will ensure a smooth transition and prevent frustration during the initial phases of AI implementation.

For example, if you're introducing an AI-powered church management system, ensure that your administrative team is fully trained to navigate the software. Similarly, if chatbots or AI-powered communication tools are being introduced, ensure that those responsible for digital outreach know how to operate, customize, and monitor these platforms.

In larger churches, designating a "tech champion" or AI liaison—someone who is comfortable with technology and willing to lead training efforts—can also be effective. This person can help onboard others, answer questions, and troubleshoot issues as they arise, ensuring a smoother transition for the entire church.

Step 5: Maintain a Focus on Ethical AI Use

One of the most important responsibilities church leaders have when adopting AI is ensuring its ethical use. AI has the capacity to gather and analyze vast amounts of data, but with that power comes the need for ethical decision-making regarding privacy, security, and transparency.

Churches often handle sensitive personal information, and any AI tool that collects or processes data must do so responsibly. This means ensuring that all AI systems comply with local data protection laws and follow best practices for privacy. Church leaders must be transparent about what data is being collected, how it is being used, and who has access to it.

In addition to privacy concerns, churches must be mindful of AI biases. Many AI systems rely on algorithms that learn from data. If that data is incomplete or biased, the AI system can unintentionally reflect those biases, leading to skewed outcomes. Regularly auditing AI systems for fairness and inclusivity is a necessary practice, particularly in diverse congregations.

Finally, AI should never be used to manipulate or coerce congregants into behavior or decisions. It is a tool meant to serve the church's mission of love and service, not control. Ethical AI implementation means maintaining the focus on human dignity and ensuring that technology enhances, rather than replaces, the personal aspects of ministry.

Step 6: Regularly Review and Adjust AI Implementation

After integrating AI tools into your church's operations, it's essential to regularly review their effectiveness. AI implementation is not a one-time process; it requires ongoing evaluation and adjustments to ensure it continues to meet the church's evolving needs.

Key metrics should be established early on to track the success of AI. These might include data on time saved in administrative tasks, increases in congregational engagement, or improvements in outreach efforts. For example, if your church adopted an AI-driven sermon preparation tool, how has it affected the amount of time pastors spend preparing? Has it improved sermon quality or congregational engagement with scripture?

Collect feedback not only from your staff but also from your congregants. AI implementation should benefit the entire church, and the perspective of the congregation can provide valuable insights into how these tools are affecting their experiences.

If areas of improvement are identified, be willing to make adjustments. Perhaps a tool that was initially helpful is no longer necessary, or new AI technologies have emerged that could better meet your needs. The field of AI is constantly evolving, and churches must remain flexible and open to change as technology advances.

Step 7: Keep Ministry at the Heart of AI Implementation

It's easy to get caught up in the excitement of technology and innovation, but at the end of the day, AI is simply a tool meant to serve a higher purpose. Church leaders must remain grounded in their mission to make disciples, spread the gospel, and build authentic relationships within their congregations.

AI should always enhance personal interactions, never replace them. Ministry is relational, and while AI can facilitate some aspects of church life, the essence of the church's work is people-focused. Pastors must ensure that AI tools do not depersonalize ministry but instead support the human connection at the heart of their calling.

Spiritual discernment is critical in this process. Just because an AI tool is available does not mean it is the right fit for your church. Pray for wisdom and seek God's guidance as you consider what technologies to adopt, always ensuring that AI serves the broader mission of glorifying God and expanding His Kingdom.

Finally, for church leaders and staff who are looking for a deeper understanding of AI technology beyond its immediate ministry applications, the companion book AI for Novices is recommended. This resource provides a technical dive into AI and offers further insights into how AI works in various fields.

Section 14.2 Training Your Team on AI Tools

The implementation of artificial intelligence in ministry presents a unique challenge: how to equip a diverse team of church staff and volunteers with the knowledge and skills to effectively use these powerful tools. This training process is crucial, as it bridges the gap between the potential of AI technology and its practical application in serving your congregation and community.

Foundational Assessment

The journey of training your team begins with a comprehensive assessment of their current knowledge and skills related to AI. This step is crucial as it allows you to tailor your training program to the specific needs of your team, ensuring that no one is left behind or bored by material they already know.

Conduct surveys to gauge familiarity with AI concepts and tools. These surveys should cover a range of topics, from basic understanding of what AI is to more specific questions about various AI applications in ministry contexts. Include questions about comfort levels with technology in general, as this can provide valuable insight into potential challenges or resistance you might face.

Follow up these surveys with one-on-one interviews with staff members. These conversations can provide deeper insights into individual concerns, interests, and learning styles. They also offer an opportunity to address any misconceptions or fears about AI that team members might have.

Consider conducting practical skills assessments as well. These involve simple tasks using AI tools to gauge current proficiency levels. For example, you might ask team members to use a basic AI chatbot or to interpret data from an AI-powered analytics tool.

Use the information gathered from these assessments to create learner profiles for your team members. These profiles can help you tailor your training approach, ensuring that each person receives the support they need to engage with AI tools effectively.

Comprehensive Curriculum Development

With a clear understanding of your team's current knowledge and skills, the next step is to develop a comprehensive training curriculum. This curriculum should cover various aspects of AI in ministry, providing both theoretical knowledge and practical skills.

Start with AI fundamentals. This section of the curriculum should cover basic concepts of artificial intelligence and machine learning. Explain how AI works at a high level, its current capabilities, and its limitations. Discuss the potential applications of AI in ministry contexts, using real-world examples to illustrate these concepts.

For instance, explain how natural language processing allows AI to understand and generate human language, and how this can be applied in creating chatbots for initial pastoral care inquiries. Or you could discuss how machine learning algorithms can analyze attendance patterns to identify members who might be disengaging from the church community.

Ethical considerations should form a crucial part of your training program. Discuss privacy and data security in AI systems, helping your team understand the importance of protecting sensitive information. Address potential biases in AI and how to mitigate them, emphasizing the need for human oversight and discernment in interpreting AI-generated insights.

Explore the theological implications of using AI in ministry. Discuss how AI aligns with your church's mission and values and where it might present challenges. Emphasize the importance of balancing AI efficiency with the human touch in ministry, ensuring that technology enhances rather than replaces personal connections.

Tool-specific training should follow these foundational modules. Provide hands-on experience with each AI tool your church is implementing. Cover best practices for using these tools in different ministry areas and how to troubleshoot common issues. This practical training will give your team the confidence to use AI tools effectively in their day-to-day work.

For example, if you're implementing an AI-powered pastoral care system, provide training on how to input data, interpret the system's recommendations, and when to override the AI's suggestions based on personal knowledge or intuition. If you're using AI for community outreach, train your team on how to use demographic analysis tools and how to craft targeted outreach strategies based on AI-generated insights.

Include sessions on AI strategy and integration in your training program. Explain how AI fits into your church's overall ministry strategy. Discuss how to integrate AI tools with existing systems and processes, and set realistic expectations for AI implementation. This strategic understanding will help your team see the bigger picture and use AI tools more purposefully.

Diverse Training Methods

To cater to different learning styles and ensure effective knowledge transfer, utilize diverse training methods. Combine in-person workshops and seminars with online courses and webinars. This blended approach allows for both real-time interaction and flexible, self-paced learning.

Create video tutorials and recorded demonstrations for those who prefer visual learning. These resources can also serve as reference materials that team members can revisit as needed. Ensure these videos are clear, concise, and focused on practical application.

Provide ample opportunities for hands-on practice. Set up sandboxed environments where team members can experiment with AI tools without fear of making mistakes that could impact real church data or operations. Encourage exploration and creativity in these practice sessions.

Implement mentoring and peer-to-peer learning programs. Identify tech-savvy team members who can serve as AI champions, providing ongoing support and guidance to their colleagues. This approach not only helps disseminate knowledge but also fosters a collaborative learning environment.

Consider gamification elements to make the learning process more engaging. Create challenges or competitions that encourage team members to apply their AI skills in creative ways. For example, you could have a contest for the most innovative use of AI in a ministry context, with prizes for the best ideas.

Ongoing Support and Continuous Learning

Remember that AI training isn't a one-time event but an ongoing process. Implement systems for continuous learning and support to ensure your team stays up-to-date with AI developments and continues to use the tools effectively.

Designate AI "champions" in each ministry area who can provide ongoing assistance to their colleagues. These champions should receive advanced training and have direct lines of communication with your AI technology providers for troubleshooting and updates.

Create an online resource library with AI tutorials, articles, and best practices that your team can access as needed. Keep this library updated with the latest information and insights about AI in ministry contexts. Encourage team members to contribute their own learnings and experiences to this knowledge base

Establish a help desk or support system for AI-related queries. This could be as simple as a dedicated email address or as sophisticated as an AI-powered chatbot that can answer common questions and direct more complex inquiries to human experts.

Schedule regular refresher training sessions to keep skills sharp and introduce new features or updates. These sessions can also serve as forums for team members to share their experiences, challenges, and successes in using AI tools.

Addressing Concerns and Resistance

Throughout the training process, be proactive in addressing any concerns or resistance to AI. Hold open forums where staff can voice their fears or misconceptions. These forums should be safe spaces where all questions and concerns are treated with respect and given thoughtful consideration.

Provide clear information about how AI will and won't be used in your church. Be transparent about the decision-making process behind AI implementation and the safeguards in place to protect privacy and ensure ethical use.

Emphasize that AI is a tool to enhance, not replace, human ministry. Use concrete examples to illustrate how AI can free up time for more personal interactions and deeper ministry work. Share success stories and positive outcomes from AI implementation to build enthusiasm and buy-in.

Address concerns about job security directly. Explain how AI is intended to augment human capabilities, not replace human roles. Discuss how team members' roles might evolve with AI implementation, focusing on the opportunities for more meaningful and impactful work.

Guidelines and Best Practices

Develop clear guidelines for AI use in your church as part of your training program. Establish protocols for data privacy and security, ensuring compliance with relevant regulations and alignment with your church's values.

Define appropriate and inappropriate uses of AI tools. For example, you might specify that AI-generated content should always be reviewed by a human before publication or that AI should not be used to make decisions about individual pastoral care without human oversight.

Create procedures for handling AI-generated insights or recommendations. Train your team on how to interpret AI outputs critically, always considering context and using their own judgment and spiritual discernment.

Develop ethical guidelines for AI use, addressing issues such as fairness, transparency, and accountability. Ensure these guidelines align with your church's mission and values, and train your team on how to apply these principles in their day-to-day use of AI tools.

Role-Specific Training

Consider creating different training tracks based on roles and responsibilities within your church. Leadership might need a higher-level strategic understanding of AI, focusing on how it can support the church's mission and vision. Those in day-to-day operations might need more hands-on technical training.

Pastoral staff should focus on how AI can enhance their ministry without replacing the essential human and spiritual elements of their work. Train them on using AI for tasks like sermon preparation, pastoral care triage, and community needs analysis.

For administrative staff, emphasize how AI can streamline operations and improve efficiency. Provide in-depth training on AI tools for tasks like scheduling, resource allocation, and financial forecasting.

For outreach and communications teams, focus on how AI can enhance their ability to connect with the community. Train them on using AI for demographic analysis, content personalization, and engagement tracking.

Real-World Application

Incorporate real-world ministry scenarios into your training. Use case studies based on actual experiences of churches using AI to illustrate both the potential and the pitfalls of these tools. Discuss how AI was implemented, what challenges were encountered, and what outcomes were achieved.

Use role-playing exercises to help your team practice applying AI tools to actual ministry situations. For example, you might simulate a pastoral care scenario where team members need to use an AI system to triage requests and determine appropriate responses.

Encourage your team to bring real challenges from their ministry areas to training sessions. Use these as opportunities for collaborative problem-solving, exploring how AI tools might be applied to address these challenges.

Measuring Effectiveness

Don't neglect the importance of measuring the effectiveness of your training program. Conducted pre-and post-training assessments to gauge improvement in AI knowledge and skills. These assessments should cover both theoretical understanding and practical application.

Gather feedback from participants after each training session. Use this feedback to continually refine and improve your training approach. Be open to suggestions for additional topics or different learning methods.

Track key performance indicators (KPIs) related to AI use in your church. These include metrics like time saved on administrative tasks, increases in community engagement, or improvements in pastoral care response times. Use these KPIs to demonstrate the tangible benefits of AI implementation and justify ongoing investment in training.

Cultivating an AI-Positive Culture

Finally, foster a culture of continuous learning and innovation around AI. Encourage your team to stay current with AI developments in ministry contexts. Share articles, podcasts, and videos about AI in ministry, and create opportunities for discussion and reflection on these resources.

Consider sending staff to relevant conferences or workshops. This not only provides additional learning opportunities but also allows your team to connect with other churches and ministries using AI, facilitating knowledge sharing and collaboration.

Create opportunities for your team to experiment with AI tools and share what they have learned with colleagues. This could involve setting aside "innovation time" where team members can explore new AI applications or hosting internal "tech showcases" where different ministry areas can demonstrate how they're using AI.

Recognize and celebrate AI successes within your church. This could involve sharing stories of how AI has enhanced ministry efforts in your church newsletter or during staff meetings. By highlighting these successes, you reinforce the value of AI and encourage continued engagement with these tools.

Remember, AI training aims not to create tech experts but to empower your team to use AI tools effectively and ethically in service of your church's mission. Keep this purpose at the forefront of your training efforts, connecting AI use to your core values and ministry objectives.

By taking a comprehensive, ongoing approach to AI training, you can ensure that your team is well-equipped to leverage artificial intelligence in ways that enhance your ministry and further your mission. This investment in training will pay dividends in more efficient operations, more effective outreach, and ultimately, a greater impact for the Kingdom of God.

As you embark on this training journey, remember the words of the Apostle Paul in Colossians 3:23-24: "Whatever you do, work at it with all your heart, as working for the Lord, not for human masters, since you know that you will receive an inheritance from the Lord as a reward. It is the Lord Christ you are serving." Let this perspective guide your approach to AI training, seeing it as part of your church's calling to steward all resources - including technology - for God's glory.

Section 14.3 Measuring the Impact of AI in Ministry

As we step into the future of AI in ministry, one critical aspect that pastors and church leaders must address is measuring its impact. Just as we assess the effectiveness of traditional ministry tools and strategies, it's essential to evaluate how AI contributes to the mission of the church. In doing so, we ensure that the integration of AI aligns with biblical principles, enhances our work, and glorifies God.

AI's potential is vast, offering opportunities to streamline administrative tasks, deepen engagement, and enhance spiritual growth. However, without proper measurement, its effectiveness remains unclear. Proverbs 27:23 reminds us to "be sure you know the condition of your flocks," emphasizing the importance of regularly assessing our efforts to shepherd God's people. This ancient wisdom guides us in this modern challenge, ensuring that AI is used not just for efficiency but for the fulfillment of the church's mission.

The Importance of Impact Measurement

Ministry work has always involved evaluation, whether through church attendance, participation in small groups, or spiritual growth metrics. Measuring the impact of AI is no different, but it requires new methods and tools given the technological nature of this field.

The true test of AI's effectiveness is in how it advances the church's mission to make disciples and minister to the community. While AI can significantly improve operations, its most valuable contribution lies in supporting the deeper spiritual goals of the church. These goals, such as nurturing faith, promoting unity, and reaching the lost, must guide how we assess AI's impact.

Moreover, church leaders need to ask: Does AI contribute to fostering a deeper relationship with Christ? Does it assist in spreading the Gospel effectively? These questions must form the foundation of any measurement framework used to evaluate AI in ministry.

Key Metrics for Measuring AI's Effectiveness

There are several key metrics that can help church leaders measure AI's impact on their ministry efforts. While AI offers many potential advantages, church leaders must ensure that these benefits are in line with their primary spiritual goals.

1. Engagement and Participation

One of the clearest indicators of AI's success in ministry is an increase in engagement and participation. AI tools, such as personalized devotional apps or sermon suggestion algorithms, can be evaluated based on how well they increase engagement with church resources.

For example, are more members attending Bible studies because of AI-driven tools? Is there an increase in the number of prayer requests or online conversations? Are members more involved in church events due to personalized reminders or tailored recommendations? These tangible signs of increased participation can offer clear insights into the effectiveness of AI.

Tracking digital engagement—such as sermon views, interaction with chatbots, and usage of Bible study apps—can give a church concrete data on how AI has improved engagement. Pastors and leaders can compare pre-AI and post-AI metrics, looking for meaningful changes in participation across various ministries.

2. Administrative Efficiency

AI's role in streamlining administrative tasks can also be a valuable metric. Metrics such as time saved in scheduling, improvements in financial management, and enhanced member communication can be easily tracked. AI-powered church management systems might reduce the workload for staff, allowing them to focus more on direct ministry.

For instance, automated tools can simplify tasks such as room scheduling, service planning, and financial management. An AI-driven financial tool might predict trends in giving, allowing church leaders to plan more effectively for future budgets. Similarly, AI can manage databases more efficiently, ensuring that congregational data is up-to-date and accurate.

The impact of these administrative improvements is not just a matter of efficiency. By freeing up time for pastors and staff to engage in direct ministry, AI indirectly fosters deeper personal connections within the congregation. Church leaders should assess how AI's administrative efficiencies contribute to the church's overall mission of pastoral care and discipleship.

3. Spiritual Growth

While spiritual growth is harder to quantify, certain AI applications can provide indicators of growth. AI-driven Bible study tools, for example, might track how frequently members engage with scripture, the variety of topics explored, or even prayer habits. Surveys or member testimonies may also provide qualitative data on how AI has supported their spiritual journey.

AI-powered platforms can offer personalized reading plans, track progress, and suggest study resources based on individual spiritual needs. This creates a tailored experience for each congregant, helping them grow in their faith. By analyzing data from these platforms, church leaders can see which spiritual resources resonate most with their congregation and adjust accordingly.

It's essential, however, that AI does not replace the personal, relational aspects of spiritual mentorship. Church leaders should evaluate whether AI tools are enhancing spiritual growth or simply making members more dependent on technology. A balanced approach ensures that while AI provides resources, the core of discipleship remains personal and Spirit-led.

4. Outreach Effectiveness

AI can also impact outreach efforts, both locally and globally. Through data analysis and AI algorithms, churches can identify and better understand the needs of their community. For instance, AI can help churches develop targeted outreach strategies, analyze social media trends, and offer personalized evangelism tools.

Churches can measure outreach success by tracking the growth of their community programs, conversion rates, or the number of new relationships formed through digital evangelism. AI can also assist in crafting more targeted, culturally relevant messages, which can improve engagement with non-churchgoers.

AI's ability to assist in real-time translation or cross-cultural communication also enables more effective global missions. When considering these global efforts, church leaders can measure success by the number of new connections made or the progress of translating scripture into new languages.

Assessing Long-Term Impacts on Ministry

As churches begin to integrate AI, it's essential to assess its long-term impact on ministry. AI is a tool that can either foster deeper relationships or potentially depersonalize interactions. Church leaders must carefully monitor whether AI is creating more meaningful connections or if it's simply automating tasks without enhancing the church's spiritual mission.

The long-term success of AI in ministry depends on its alignment with the church's core values. For example, does AI help build a stronger sense of community? Does it foster greater empathy and understanding among congregants? Church leaders should regularly assess the relational and spiritual outcomes of AI implementation to ensure it serves the church's mission.

Ethical Considerations in Measurement

When implementing and measuring AI's impact, ethical considerations are paramount. Church leaders should ensure that data collected through AI is handled responsibly. This includes respecting privacy, ensuring transparency, and avoiding manipulation. James 3:17 reminds us that wisdom is "pure, peaceable, gentle," and ethical AI practices must reflect these values in ministry.

Data privacy is a significant concern in any context where personal information is collected, and churches are no exception. Church leaders must establish clear policies for handling congregational data and ensure that AI systems are compliant with data protection laws. Additionally, AI should be used to empower, not control, the congregation's spiritual journey.

Furthermore, the risk of AI depersonalizing pastoral care must be addressed. While AI can handle administrative tasks and provide analytical insights, it cannot replace the deeply relational aspects of ministry. Church leaders should be mindful of maintaining genuine, personal relationships even while utilizing AI's capabilities.

Another ethical consideration is algorithmic bias, where AI may unintentionally favor certain groups over others based on the data it receives. Ensuring that AI tools are inclusive and fair is vital, especially in diverse congregations where people come from various cultural, social, and economic backgrounds.

Practical Steps for Measuring AI Impact

Churches looking to measure the impact of AI should start by setting clear, measurable goals. Whether the goal is to increase Bible study participation or improve community outreach, having specific benchmarks allows leaders to track progress over time. Regular evaluations and adjustments ensure that AI tools remain effective and relevant to the ministry's needs.

Churches can implement surveys, focus groups, and data analytics to gather feedback on AI tools from the congregation. These insights will help refine AI applications and ensure that they meet the community's spiritual and practical needs. Regular reviews of AI's impact should become a part of the church's strategic planning process.

As AI continues to shape the future of ministry, church leaders have a responsibility to assess its impact thoughtfully. AI is not a silver bullet, nor is it meant to replace the human touch in ministry. However, when used correctly, it can be a powerful tool for advancing the church's mission to glorify God and serve His people.

By measuring engagement, efficiency, spiritual growth, and outreach success, leaders can ensure AI is a tool that empowers, rather than detracts from, their efforts. Moreover, ethical considerations, including data privacy and algorithmic fairness, must always guide the use of AI in ministry contexts.

AI will likely introduce even more powerful tools and strategies for ministry. It is essential to continually measure its effectiveness and adjust accordingly, always remembering that technology is a means to serve a higher calling. AI should support the church's mission, not redefine it.

Ultimately, the future of AI in ministry is bright, but its success depends on how well church leaders can integrate this technology into their spiritual vision. If AI is used prayerfully and intentionally, its impact can be profound, enabling churches to reach more people and deepen the faith of their communities.

Epilogue

Concluding AI for Ministry invites reflection on the journey through these chapters and the deeper message the book seeks to convey. Artificial intelligence (AI) has undeniably permeated every aspect of society, including ministry. Yet, merely recognizing AI's presence is insufficient. The true challenge lies in harnessing its power in ways that align with our mission as followers of Christ and stewards of His church.

The use of AI in ministry is not just about leveraging new technologies to improve administrative efficiency, streamline tasks, or engage with our congregations more effectively. It is fundamentally about ensuring that we are faithful to the Great Commission in the digital age.

As we move forward, church leaders and pastors need to be both wise and discerning, understanding that while AI holds immense potential, it must never supersede the personal, relational, and spiritual aspects of our work. Ministry, at its core, is about people, relationships, and our collective journey toward Christ. AI should be a tool that supports that mission, not a replacement for human connection.

A Call to Discernment in the Digital Age

One of the central themes that this book has underscored is the need for discernment. AI can automate processes, provide insights, and even engage with individuals in a personalized manner. However, without a strong ethical and theological foundation, we run the risk of allowing technology to dictate how we approach ministry. Instead of allowing AI to determine our direction, we must ensure that it is aligned with biblical principles and guided by our mission to glorify God and make disciples.

As we discussed in earlier chapters, discernment is particularly crucial when addressing issues of data privacy, ethical AI implementation, and algorithmic biases. The church has always been called to uphold justice and truth, and this must extend into how we handle the technology we employ. AI can be an incredible tool for outreach, pastoral care, and education, but we must ensure that we use it responsibly. Church leaders are responsible for guarding the privacy and dignity of their congregants, ensuring that the data AI collects is used ethically and transparently.

Moreover, as AI becomes more integrated into our ministries, we must be aware of the potential for dehumanization. The convenience and efficiency of AI should never replace the relational, incarnational nature of Christian ministry. Jesus Himself demonstrated a ministry that was deeply personal—focused on individuals, relationships, and community. In a world increasingly driven by technology, the church must remain grounded in this relational model, using AI to enhance, not replace, personal connection.

The Role of AI in Spiritual Growth

Another key area of exploration in this book has been the role of AI in fostering spiritual growth. We have seen how AI can assist believers in their spiritual journey, from AI-driven Bible study tools to personalized devotional apps. However, it is essential to remember that spiritual growth is a deeply personal and Spirit-led process. AI can help us engage more deeply with scripture, provide tools for reflection, and offer guidance, but it cannot replace the work of the Holy Spirit in transforming hearts.

The goal of spiritual growth in the Christian life is not merely knowledge or engagement but transformation—becoming more like Christ in character and action. AI can provide resources and tools, but it cannot replace the personal work of discipleship that takes place in the context of community. Therefore, pastors and church leaders must be mindful of how they integrate AI into discipleship programs. AI should be a supplement to human mentorship, pastoral care, and the fellowship of believers, not a substitute for them.

In this respect, one of the book's key takeaways is the need for balance. As AI tools continue to develop, they will undoubtedly become more sophisticated, offering even more personalized spiritual resources. Church leaders must continually evaluate whether these tools are truly fostering deeper spiritual engagement or merely creating a veneer of growth. Genuine transformation comes from a life surrendered to Christ, and while AI can facilitate that journey, it cannot replace the relationship between the believer and God.

The Future of AI in Ministry: Opportunities and Challenges

Looking toward the future, AI presents both opportunities and challenges for the church. Throughout this book, we have explored practical ways that AI can assist in various aspects of ministry— from sermon preparation to pastoral care, from worship to evangelism. The opportunities AI provides are exciting, and it is clear that we are only at the beginning of understanding how this technology can transform ministry.

One of the most significant opportunities AI offers is its ability to enhance outreach and evangelism. As discussed in Chapter 11, AI can analyze vast amounts

485

of data to help churches understand their communities better and develop targeted outreach strategies. AI's ability to process and interpret data from social media, demographic trends, and even online interactions allows churches to be more intentional in how they reach out to the unchurched or those who may be seeking spiritual guidance.

However, with these opportunities come significant challenges. One of the greatest challenges is ensuring that AI does not alienate or marginalize those who may not have access to or understanding of technology. The digital divide is a real concern, and as church leaders adopt AI tools, they must be mindful of those within their congregations or communities who may be excluded from participating in these new initiatives due to a lack of technological access or literacy.

Moreover, as AI becomes more ingrained in ministry, church leaders must navigate the fine line between efficiency and dependency. It is easy to become overly reliant on AI for tasks that should remain in the hands of human pastors and leaders—tasks like counseling, discipleship, and spiritual guidance. AI can assist in these areas, but it cannot replace the empathy, wisdom, and relational depth that come from human interaction.

Keeping Ministry Human in a Digital Age

The central message of AI for Ministry has been that AI, while a powerful tool, must never replace the human element of ministry. Ministry is about relationships—relationships with God, with fellow believers, and with the world around us. AI can enhance our ability to connect, communicate, and serve, but it should always be seen as a tool to support human effort, not replace it.

As we move further into the digital age, the temptation will be to let technology take the lead in many aspects of our lives, including ministry. However, the church's mission has always been to serve people, not technology. AI can be a valuable asset in helping us reach people, but it must be used in a way that preserves the relational and incarnational nature of the Gospel.

Pastors and church leaders must continue to prioritize face-to-face interactions, personal relationships, and community-building efforts. As helpful as AI may be, it cannot replicate the experience of sitting with someone in their grief, sharing in their joy, or walking with them in their spiritual journey. Ministry is deeply human, and while AI can assist in many ways, it cannot replace the love, compassion, and care that define the work of the church.

A Final Word on Stewardship

Throughout this book, the theme of stewardship has surfaced repeatedly. Stewardship is about more than managing resources wisely; it is about faithfully using all that God has entrusted to us for His glory and the good of others. As we integrate AI into our ministries, we must view it as a form of stewardship. God has given us the opportunity to use this powerful technology to advance His Kingdom, and we are responsible for using it wisely.

This means that church leaders must continually ask themselves: Are we using AI in a way that glorifies God? Are we serving our congregation and community faithfully with the tools we have? Are we ensuring that AI supports our mission rather than distracts from it?

Stewardship also means recognizing that technology is not a substitute for the work of the Holy Spirit. No matter how advanced AI becomes, it will never replace the need for prayer, discernment, and reliance on God's guidance. The church must always remain rooted in the knowledge that our strength comes from God, not from human invention. AI is a tool that can enhance our work, but it is God who ultimately brings about transformation, growth, and renewal in His people.

Looking Forward: AI as a Tool for the Kingdom

As we wrap up this book, I hope you, the reader, have gained a deeper understanding of how AI can be used effectively and faithfully in ministry. AI's potential is vast, and its future applications in the church are exciting. However, the success of AI in ministry will depend on how well church leaders can balance the use of technology with the church's core mission.

AI is not an end in itself. It is a means to an end—the end being the glorification of God and the advancement of His Kingdom. As long as we keep this focus in mind, AI can be a powerful tool for serving others, spreading the Gospel, and helping people grow in their relationship with Christ.

For those who wish to dive deeper into the technical aspects of artificial intelligence, I encourage you to explore the companion book AI for Novices. While AI for Ministry provides practical guidance for pastors and church leaders, AI for Novices offers a deeper technical understanding of the various AI tools and systems available today. It is an excellent resource for those looking to build a more comprehensive understanding of AI's inner workings and applications beyond ministry.

In closing, I encourage you to approach AI with both excitement and caution. Embrace the opportunities it offers but remain grounded in the unchanging truths of Scripture. Remember that while AI can assist in many aspects of ministry, the heart of ministry is about relationships—relationships that are built through love, care, and the guidance of the Holy Spirit.

As we move into the future, may we use every tool at our disposal—including AI—to fulfill the call of Christ to make disciples of all nations. Let us approach this new frontier with wisdom, discernment, and a steadfast commitment to the Gospel, always seeking to glorify God in all that we do.

Resources

Recommended Books

- Mere Christianity by C.S. Lewis
- The Local Church Today by Bill Scheidler
- Principles of Church Life by Bill Scheidler
- Every Good Endeavor by Timothy Keller
- Beyond Opinion by Ravi Zacharias
- Issues Facing Christians Today by John Stott
- The Knowledge of the Holy by A.W. Tozer
- The Holiness of God by R.C. Sproul
- Next Step series (1.0, 2.0, 3.0) by Bill Scheidler
- Technopoly: The Surrender of Culture to Technology by Neil Postman
- The Shallows: What the Internet is Doing to Our Brains by Nicholas Carr
- God, Technology, and the Christian Life by Tony Reinke
- AI Superpowers: China, Silicon Valley, and the New World Order by Kai-Fu Lee
- The Second Machine Age: Work, Progress, and Prosperity in a Time of Brilliant Technologies by Erik Brynjolfsson and Andrew McAfee

Online Resources

- Bible Study & Theology
  - Church Leadership Resources by Bill Scheidler: www.churchleadershipresources.com
  - The Bible Project: www.bibleproject.com
  - Blue Letter Bible: www.blueletterbible.org
  - Logos Bible Software: www.logos.com
  - Bible Gateway: www.biblegateway.com
- Artificial Intelligence & Ethics
  - Future of Life Institute: www.futureoflife.org
  - AI & Faith: www.aiandfaith.org
  - Partnership on AI: www.partnershiponai.org
- Christian Education
  - Biblical Training: www.churchleadershipresources.com
  - Regent University: www.regent.edu
- Church Management Tools
  - Faithlife Equip: www.faithlife.com/products/equip
  - Planning Center: www.planningcenter.com

Educational Websites and Courses

- AI & Ministry Courses
    - Coursera AI for Everyone:
      www.coursera.org/learn/ai-for-everyone
    - edX Artificial Intelligence Programs:
      www.edx.org/course/artificial-intelligence
    - FaithTech: www.faithtech.com
- General Christian Education
    - BiblicalTraining.org:
      www.biblicaltraining.org
    - Online Theological Training:
      www.biblicaltraining.org
    - Regent University: www.regent.edu

Sermon and Bible Study Tools

- SermonCentral: www.sermoncentral.com
- YouVersion Bible App: www.youversion.com
- Bible Study Fellowship (BSF):
  www.bsfinternational.org

AI-Specific Tools for Ministry

- Faithlife Equip for Church Management:
  www.faithlife.com/products/equip
- Planning Center: www.planningcenter.com
- Logos AI tools for sermon preparation and
  exegesis: www.logos.com

Podcasts & Media

- Ask Pastor John (by John Piper):
  www.desiringgod.org/ask-pastor-john
- RZIM Let My People Think (Ravi Zacharias):
  www.rzim.org/listen/let-my-people-think
- The Gospel Coalition Podcast:
  www.thegospelcoalition.org/podcasts
- The Bible for Normal People Podcast:
  www.thebiblefornormalpeople.com
- Bill Scheidler's Podcast (School of Ministry):
  tinyurl.com/SchoolMinistry

Ministry and Leadership Resources

- Barna Research: www.barna.com
- Lifeway Leadership:
  www.lifeway.com/en/shop/leadership
- Church Leadership Resources by Bill
  Scheidler:
  www.churchleadershipresources.com

About the Author

Jeremy Wheeler is a seasoned software architect and ministry leader based in Vancouver, WA, with over 30 years of experience in the IT industry. Throughout his career, Jeremy has been a forward-thinker, constantly seeking to push the boundaries of technology while staying grounded in his faith. His technical expertise has allowed him to impact various industries, but his true passion lies in ministry and helping others find freedom and purpose in Christ.

Jeremy's personal journey has cultivated a deep passion to see people set free from bondage and walk in the fullness of Christ. Out of that burden, he founded FightLust.com to equip believers with gospel-centered resources, accountability frameworks, and practical tools for lasting freedom. Drawing on Scripture, pastoral care principles, and community support, the ministry helps people move from shame to Spirit-led wholeness in Jesus.

In addition to FightLust.com, Jeremy serves as a board member at The Remnant Barn, a ministry that brings together worshipers from various churches and denominations to foster unity and community. His leadership extends to Worship Encounter, a powerful series of worship events that create a space for believers to encounter God's presence in a deep and transformative way. These events focus on Spirit-led worship, breaking down barriers, and bringing people into a closer relationship with God.

Beyond his ministry work, Jeremy has a passion for making complex technologies accessible to everyone. His book, AI for Novices, simplifies the world of artificial intelligence, making it understandable for those who are new to the field. Through his writing, Jeremy aims to demystify AI and show how it can be used for good in everyday life, helping readers engage with technology in a meaningful way.

Jeremy's journey is a testament to God's power to transform lives. Whether through his technical work or his ministry, Jeremy is committed to serving others, encouraging them to experience the freedom that comes from a relationship with Jesus Christ. He continues to inspire those around him to embrace their God-given purpose and live lives of victory and peace.